MAPLE LEAF GARDENS

Fifty Years of History

STAN OBODIAC

Van Nostrand Reinhold Ltd., Toronto,
New York, Cincinnati, London, Melbourne

Published in Canada by Van Nostrand Reinhold Ltd., Toronto. Published simultaneously in the United States of America by Van Nostrand Reinhold Company, New York.

Library of Congress Catalogue Number 81-50745

CANADIAN CATALOGUING IN PUBLICATION DATA
Obodiac, Stan, 1922-
    Maple Leaf Gardens

ISBN 0-442-29635-5

1. Maple Leaf Gardens — History.   2. Toronto (Ont.) —
Sports facilities.   I. Title.

GV416.T67O26   796'.06'8209713541   C81-094629-7

EDITORIAL CONSULTANT: James T. Wills
DESIGN: Brant Cowie/Artplus Ltd.
COVER PHOTOGRAPHS: *Top:* A line-up in the 1930s (Pringle & Booth Limited); *Left and right:* Tennis at the Gardens (Jerry Hobbs); *Centre left:* Elvis Presley (Alexandra Studio); *Centre right:* Ace Frehley of Kiss (Peter Coriglione); *Centre:* Darryl Sittler (Dennis Miles)
TYPESETTING: Compeer Typographic Services Limited

Printed and bound in Canada by The Bryant Press Limited

81 82 83 84 85 86 87 7 6 5 4 3 2 1

ACKNOWLEDGMENTS

My thanks to Nancy Ryder, Gord Finn and Irwin "Patty" Patoff for recording in the box office the significant events that appear in the Chronology. I would also like to thank the photographers whose photographs appear in the book and the people and companies that provided photographs and information, in particular, Harold Ballard, Garden Brothers Circus, Ice Follies, Ice Capades, Johnny Lombardi, Charles Templeton, Frank Tunney, Irv Ungerman and Fred Waldon.

Every possible care has been taken to correctly acknowledge copyright information. The author and publisher would welcome information that will enable them to rectify any errors or omissions in succeeding printings.

To all the people who have patronized Maple Leaf Gardens
throughout the building's fifty-year history, I say thank you.
Now we must go on to the new year, and the next fifty years.

HAROLD E. BALLARD

*Former Lieutenant-Governor of
Ontario, Pauline McGibbon, drops
the puck between Stan Mikita and
Darryl Sittler, October 11, 1975.*
ROBERT SHAVER

Contents

BOX   ROW   SEAT

40   A   4

WEST

Retain Stub — Good Only

(38)

SAT. MAR. 14

8.00 P.M.   1981

Davis Printing Limited

WASHINGTON CAPITALS
VS.
TORONTO MAPLE LEAFS

ADMIT ONE. Entrance by Main Door or by West Door, Carlton St.

Maple Leaf Gardens
LIMITED

CONDITION OF SALE

Upon refunding the purchase price the management may remove from the premises any person who has obtained admission by this ticket.

40   **A**   **4**

NATIONAL HOCKEY LEAGUE

PRICE 13.64 + RST 1.36 15.00

SAT., MAR. 14, 1981

A PAIR OF GOLDS

MAPLE LEAF GARDENS has an enviable and incredible sports attendance record. Since 1946 there hasn't been a single unsold ticket for a National Hockey League hockey game — nearly thirty-five years of continuous sell-outs.

A pair of tickets to a hockey game, no matter where in the building the seats happen to be, is a prestige item across the entire country. Tickets are so much in demand that they have often sold for as much as $250 a pair, although regular prices are only $15 for hockey. Stories have been told of people who have offered a new car or membership in the Royal Yacht Club for season tickets. In fact, people used to leave them in their wills. One account relates that a divorce suit was settled over a pair of hockey tickets — you keep the car, I'll keep the tickets.

Visiting princes, ambassadors, prime ministers, government officials, celebrities — any time they are in the city, hockey tickets are usually in order, but only the best, a pair of golds.

In 1980 there were 6,500 people on the season ticket waiting list, even though many Ontarians went to Buffalo for tickets when that city was granted a National Hockey League franchise. The tremendous appetite for hockey is matched on occasion by modern music shows and other attractions at the Gardens. But no matter what the event, a pair of seats at Maple Leaf Gardens has been one of the most desired sets of tickets in Canada over the past fifty years; they are a gilded passport to some of the finest entertainment in the world.

A 1931 line-up outside the newly completed Gardens.
PRINGLE & BOOTH LIMITED

CHAPTER I   BUILDING THE GARDENS

OVER THE PAST FIFTY YEARS, many changes have occurred near the corner of Carlton and Church in Toronto. The entire skyline of the area has been altered. One thing remains constant, though: Maple Leaf Gardens, now just a short walk from the gleaming Eaton Centre and the bustle of Canada's Yonge Street strip. Nearly 100 million people have stopped in to be entertained at the Gardens in the last half-century. Countless millions have paused just to have a look at the place that has become something of a legend in Canada and indeed across North America.

Even the site of the building has historical significance. A decisive battle was fought on the spot during the Rebellion of 1837; Sheriff Jarvis fired on William Lyon Mackenzie's insurgents and halted them there. But the Gardens was not founded on rebellion, it was founded on hockey. By 1930, before the Gardens was constructed, over two million fans had already seen National Hockey League games, and the sport was growing in popularity. In Toronto, two professional teams, the Toronto Arenas and the St. Pats, played out of the old Mutual Street arena. These were exciting teams to watch, and in fact, the Arenas won the Stanley Cup in 1917, their first year of operation and the first year of the NHL.

The popularity of these teams meant that the Mutual Street rink couldn't accommodate the crowds. The St. Pats had become the Toronto Maple Leafs in 1927, and by 1931 the managing director of the team, Conn Smythe, was faced with a decision: either give up pro hockey in the city or get along by selling a few players and operating as cheaply as possible. Neither alternative was suitable. Smythe, the son of a Hamilton newspaperman, once remarked that, "I was sired by an Irishman and dammed by an Englishwoman. I've got my father's fight and my mother's common sense," and predictably he took a third course. After reading the ecstatic accounts of the building of the Empire State Building, which opened in New York in May 1931, he decided that his team and the city should have their own building.

Conn Smythe was a businessman, but he was also concerned with the welfare of others. He felt that housing the team on Mutual Street wasn't fair to the players. "If they were playing for New York or Boston or Chicago or any other team in the league," he observed during a Mutual Street practice, "they'd be getting higher salaries than we're paying. Besides, we aren't making much money for ourselves, even if we get in the playoffs. The arena seats around 8,000; what we need to be fair to the players, fans and owners is a rink that will hold at least 12,000." This kind of observation was typical of Smythe; he put the welfare of his players before his business interests.

Foster Hewitt undoubtedly did more than anyone else in Canada to popularize both the sport and Maple Leaf Gardens, but it is not commonly known that his image among the fans played a major role in the final decision to proceed with the construction of the building. Foster's story has been told many times: how he began working for the *Toronto Daily Star* in 1922 at the age of eighteen, and then in 1923 broadcast his first senior league game between Parkdale and Kitchener. Foster soon began broadcasting NHL games over radio station CFCA from the Mutual Street arena. His distinctive style and his trademark "He shoots! He scores!" made the game so popular in an already hockey-crazy town that Conn Smythe asked him to join the team organization. The agreement was concluded before the Gardens' construction started, and no doubt Smythe was confident that Hewitt would help fill the new building. Their professional relationship continued for many years.

Building a new arena was not an easy task. The effects of the Great Depression were deepening, the team had few resources and appropriate land was not easy to find. Above all, the Mutual Street management was demanding that the Leafs pay $1,000 for any home games played elsewhere prior to 1932. Even more of a problem, however, was the fact that it was estimated a new arena would cost $1.5 million.

But Smythe had help, initially in the form of advice from Toronto businessmen Larkin Maloney, Alfred Rogers, J. P. Bickell and Ed Bickle and from his assistant Frank Selke, Sr. Smythe put together a 1930 souvenir hockey programme outlining his plans for a new building. Hewitt promoted the programme on his broadcasts, asking fans to send in ten cents for a copy, thereby getting a reliable indication of interest in the concept. The response was overwhelming and encouraged Smythe to take the next step — selling stock in the venture. Smythe's friends were among the first to subscribe, affording him enough of a cash flow to launch the project.

His mind made up, and confident that more money could be found despite the Depression, Smythe began to look for land. His first choice was a location on the Lake Ontario waterfront close to Yonge and Fleet streets. There he planned to have a large parking lot with a tunnel leading directly into the rink, a boon for wintertime hockey fans. However, the land was not available for outright purchase.

The "Gardens" Executive

Harry McGee
G. R. Cottrelle
J. P. Bickell
E. W. Bickle
Conn Smythe

Directors of Maple Leaf Gardens, Limited

SIR JOHN AIRD   MR. R. A. LAIDLAW   MR. ALFRED ROGERS
MR. J. P. BICKELL   MR. W. A. H. MacBRIEN   MR. FRANK A. ROLPH
MR. E. W. BICKLE   MR. LEIGHTON McCARTHY   MR. VICTOR ROSS
MR. J. E. BIRKS   MR. HARRY McGEE   HON. W. D. ROSS
MR. G. R. COTTRELLE   MR. F. K. MORROW   MR. R. HOME SMITH
MR. A. L. ELLSWORTH   MR. J. Y. MURDOCH   MR. CONN SMYTHE
MR. GEO. H. GOODERHAM MR. FRANK P. O'CONNOR   MR. JOHN A. TORY

ABOVE: *The skeleton of the Gardens takes shape in the summer of 1931.*
W. S. OLIPHANT

RIGHT: *This picture of the businessmen who helped Conn Smythe raise money to build the Gardens appeared in the first hockey programme.*

He then looked at a location on Spadina Avenue. It had been proposed that Knox College, then on Spadina, should be torn down. But local residents, led by Alderman Nathan Phillips, opposed the demolition and that plan was also put to rest. It is interesting to speculate on the contemporary look of either of these areas had one of Smythe's approaches been successful.

After this discouraging start, Eaton's became involved. Smythe approached the company and found that they were interested in selling a plot of land for a new arena. Eaton's had recently opened their College Street store, and originally they seemed to feel that a new ice rink would bring potential customers to the area. To this end, they offered a block north of Wood Street. Smythe, on the other hand, wanted a block at the corner of Church and Carlton streets. First of all, he felt that the land was underpriced at $350,000. Secondly, it was located on streetcar lines and offered easy access to the fans. This wasn't as good as a parking lot with a tunnel, but it would do. Finally, Smythe was interested because the site was only a stone's throw from his birthplace.

Smythe won, but it wasn't an easy battle. He delegated Ed Bickle to approach J. J. Vaughan of Eaton's about the Church-Carlton block. Bickle ran up against a stone wall. "He said Eaton's did not want a hockey arena so close to their spacious College Street store," Frank Selke wrote. "The people who attended sports events were hardly the type to whom Eaton's catered." This was certainly contradictory to earlier encouragements, but in the end Vaughan saw that the Gardens could be helpful to business. Bickle not only obtained an option on the land, he also sold Eaton's $25,000 worth of Gardens' stock.

Now the land was there waiting. All Smythe needed was the money to buy the option and build the rink. So he began knocking on doors. Bankers were offered the security of a good investment and profits. The city was approached with the idea that Toronto would have a major arena to be proud of and call its own, one that might also attract conventions. The unions were swayed by the opportunity for employment. Smythe was even successful in obtaining money from some of Canada's leading industries.

Despite the Depression, the land was purchased and preparations began. The old houses and stores at the corner of Church and Carlton were demolished beginning on April 1, 1931. Thomson Brothers Construction Company won the building contract, and construction began on May 1. The large number of unemployed workers at the time and the fact that costs were twenty to thirty percent lower than they had been a few years earlier made it possible to erect the building in five months.

At various times 1,300 men were employed on the project. A total of 750,000 bricks were used, as well as 77,500 bags of cement, 70 tons

The corner of Carlton and Church, with opening night only two months away.

At the first charity game at the Gardens, January 21, 1933, the Toronto Maple Leafs defeated four amateur teams.
PRINGLE & BOOTH LIMITED

The Gardens offered complete sports facilities, including a bowling alley. Toronto Mayor Sam McBride throws the first ball to open a tournament in the 1930s.
ALEXANDRA STUDIO

The interior of the south press box during a Leafs' game in the 1950s.
GRAPHIC ARTISTS

Maple Leaf Gardens was the first arena in the world to flood the ice between periods. Former building superintendent Doug Morris (right) prepares the original ice resurfacing machine, which is now on display at the Gardens.
ALEXANDRA STUDIO

of sand, 1,100 tons of gravel, 950,000 board-feet of lumber, 540 kegs of nails, and 230,000 haylite blocks. Workers hung a timer's clock over the ice surface that weighed 10,000 pounds. Fourteen miles of pipe were laid below the concrete floor to carry the 16,000 gallons of brine that would be needed to make ice. The ice-making machines were installed that would chill the brine to temperatures as low as −28°F. (−33°C.), allowing the surface to hold an inch-and-a-half of ice after the floor had been sprayed sixteen times with fine mist. When the building was finally finished, it towered thirteen stories above street level.

The new arena took up 350 feet on Carlton Street and 282 feet on Church. Attractive stores were incorporated into the outside ground level, and all in all the Gardens was an imposing addition to the mid-Depression development of downtown Toronto.

To the Toronto Maple Leafs of the day, the building looked like a palace, especially after playing within the confines of the Mutual Street shinny rink. As King Clancy, a former hockey player and now Vice President of the Maple Leaf Hockey Club and the Hamilton Tiger Cat Football Club, recalls, the first place the players wanted to see was the dressing room. Mutual Street had hot water in the showers but only as long as someone didn't use it all, but at the Gardens — well, hot water was in plentiful supply.

The building was officially opened at 8:30 p.m. on November 12, 1931 with a hockey game that was played to a full house of 13,233. The 48th Highlanders and the Royal Grenadiers struck up "Happy Days Are Here Again," the Leafs were given floral horseshoes and the crowd hooted at the lengthy speeches of the likes of Ed Bickle. The Leafs, with hockey immortals Lorne Chabot, Reginald "Red" Horner, King Clancy and the youthful "Kid Line" of Charlie Conacher, Joe Primeau and Harvey "Busher" Jackson lost 2-1 to the Chicago Black Hawks, but the opening was a huge success. The players loved the arena and the fans loved it too. The crowd was the largest to see a sporting event up to that time in Toronto, and the gross gate was $19,677.50, based on seat prices of $2.75, $1.85, $1.40, and 95 cents.

But if the Gardens was constructed to serve the team and the public, it also rewarded those who had worked on it. Because Conn Smythe was still short about $200,000 when the project began, the construction workers were persuaded to accept twenty percent of their pay in stock, as were some contractors and suppliers. This agreement has paid handsomely for those who have retained their certificates. The original preferred share was valued at $10, and each worker was given one free share for each five shares of common stock that he owned. Preferred shares eventually rose to $12.50 and common stock to over $80 each, before the shares were split four to one and then three to one.

The Gardens originally held 13,500 spectators for hockey and 16,000 for other attractions. At first, it contained a bowling alley, a billiards room and a gymnasium. It was big, so big in fact, that a 1964 *Maclean's* article about a 228 million-bushel sale of wheat to Russia mentioned that the grain would fill the Gardens nearly 5,500 times. The figure was inaccurate, because the building contains thirteen million cubic feet and the wheat would only fill it twenty-two times. Still, the comparison does give an idea of how big the Gardens really is, and in the Depression days, before the modern skyscrapers were built, it looked even bigger.

Over the years there have been a number of physical changes to the building. One of the most important and least obvious occurs every time a different event takes place on the arena floor. Unlike ice for hockey games, for instance, which can vary slightly from end to end, curling ice, such as that prepared for the Tournament of Champions held in 1964, must be completely level. In addition, different temperatures of brine in the freezing pipes, varying air temperatures and the size of the crowd can cause marked changes in curling ice. A major tournament could turn into a disaster if the maintenance workers weren't on their toes.

The highlight of the 1955-56 season was the installation of four new Turnbull escalators, the first of their kind in any North American sports arena. With two on the east side and two on the west, these reversible escalators could handle 20,000 people per hour. According to the manufacturer, they were "the latest word in comfortable, safe transportation."

When the highly prized gold seats were introduced into the building in 1974, comedian Johnny Wayne had the following comment: "I'll tell you something funny about the seats. My two sons and I measured the gold seats recently. They're two inches wider than the greys. This building must have been built on the premise that if you're rich, you've got a big behind."

It wasn't long ago, 1979 to be exact, that Foster Hewitt's gondola was replaced with a new broadcast booth. Many people felt that the gondola should be preserved for posterity as a symbol of hockey tradition, but it was dismantled.

Escalators, gold seats and other improvements must have made some difference because in 1978 there were 290 attractions in 365 days, including 50 pro hockey games, 50 rock shows and 34 ice show performances. Of the 16,307 seats and 178 standing room spaces available in the building by this time, most were filled for the majority of events.

Many of these innovations came about as the result of building ownership changes during the 1960s. In 1957, Conn Smythe created the hockey committee known as the "Silver Seven," including John Bassett, Harold Ballard and Stafford Smythe, among others. They made decisions on all matters affecting the Leafs and, their junior league team, the Toronto Marlboros.

ABOVE: *An early photograph of hockey broadcaster, Foster Hewitt.* CHARLES AYLETT

RIGHT: *A page of Lou Skuce cartoons from the first hockey programme.*

As Our Radio Friends See Us

Conn Smythe (seated, centre) retired on November 23, 1961. Included in this picture, taken at Smythe's last meeting with the Gardens' executive, are Stafford Smythe (seated to the right of his father), John Bassett (seated third from left), George Mara (seated first from right) and Harold Ballard (seated second from right).
ALEXANDRA STUDIO

Horace Lapp, an organist at the Gardens during the 1950s.
GRAPHIC ARTISTS

From 1931 to 1981, the Leafs' equipment man, Tommy Nayler, introduced many innovations in hockey equipment.

The Hot Stove Club.

Ballard, Bassett and Stafford Smythe decided to try to gain control of the building, and they started buying up stock. Conn Smythe found out and became understandably angry with his son, Staff. However, Ballard and Bassett continued to purchase stock on the verbal agreement that shares would be equalized among the three partners: the elder Smythe, Bassett and Ballard. The crisis came in 1961. As Harold Ballard described it to John Gault in a *Toronto Life* interview, Ballard found out that some 14,000 shares of Gardens' stock were about to come on the market. "I was in the board room," Ballard recalled, "and I heard Staff and his father and Fred Crawford [Director at the time] talking about how they were going to buy the whole 14,000 for $24.50 each. My ears turned around like a donkey's, and I ran out of the board room to a pay phone and called Bassett at the "Tely" [*The Toronto Telegram*]. He phoned the trust company and offered $25 a share for the whole keboodle and we bought it all."

Later, Ballard was able to come up with $2.5 million to buy out Conn. Bassett became Chairman of the Board, Staff Smythe President and Ballard Executive Vice-President. In September, 1971, Bassett in turn sold his stock to Ballard and Stafford Smythe, receiving among other things $5.4 million for an initial investment of $900,000.

All went relatively smoothly under the new regime until August 31, 1968, when an auditor's report noted a discrepancy in Gardens' funds allocated for construction. Stafford Smythe died on October 13, 1971, after he and Ballard were investigated for the discrepancy. In early February, 1972, Harold Ballard was able to gain undisputed control of the Gardens, when he purchased $7.5 million worth of shares from Stafford Smythe's estate.

These and many other important events have occurred at the Gardens during the last half-century, and many important people have entered the doors at Carlton and Church to entertain and to be entertained. It would be impossible to discuss in detail anything but the high points in a book of manageable size, and for this reason a Chronology appears at the back of the book that lists the important events and personalities.

There has been hockey, of course, and the Toronto Maple Leafs have brought eleven Stanley Cups to the building, the first in 1932, and the last in 1967. It has always been the major sport, and before the advent of television millions of Canadians listened to Foster Hewitt call the play-by-play on radio. Names like Charlie Conacher, King Clancy, Joe Primeau, Syl Apps and Ted "Teeder" Kennedy became household words because of Foster's descriptions of their exploits on the Gardens' ice. What fan can forget the great Leaf games, or the Marlboros, or the electrifying international games played under the Gardens' roof?

The Gardens has also hosted many other sports: wrestling, boxing, tennis, swimming, track and field, curling, bowling and lacrosse, to name but a few. In fact, most sports have been played in the build-

Two Presidents of Maple Leaf Gardens, Conn Smythe and Harold Ballard. This picture, taken at the 1980 Sports Celebrity Dinner, also marked Smythe's eighty-fifth birthday.
JERRY HOBBS

ing over the past fifty years. Frank Tunney's wrestling matches introduced such names as Whipper Billy Watson, The Masked Marvel and Haystack Calhoun to the wrestling fan. Gardens' boxing cards have featured great fighters like Floyd Patterson, George Chuvalo and Muhammad Ali. The first National Basketball Association game was played at the Gardens, while tennis stars of the calibre of Bill Tilden, Pancho Gonzales, Jimmy Connors, Ilie Nastase and Bjorn Borg have thrilled audiences.

Amateur sport has not been ignored. The years of the Second World War saw an increase in the number of amateur events held in the building, including many sponsored by the military. This trend continued after peace was declared, particularly in track and field, hockey and gymnastics.

All in all the Gardens has developed a strong sporting tradition not only within its walls but also across Canada. The amateur and the professional alike dreams of the day that an appearance in Canada's premier sports arena will be possible.

The Gardens has always been versatile, and its presentations do not stop with sports. There was an entire decade when some of the world's greatest operas and ballets were staged. Frank Sinatra and Bob Hope have appeared there, as well as the great stars of rock music, beginning with Bill Haley and his Comets. Bingo games, dances, concerts, religious meetings and political rallies only begin to round out the numerous kinds of events held in the building.

Great personalities from all walks of life have added to the fame of the Gardens: Winston Churchill, lecturing in 1933 before he made his indelible mark on world history; R. B. Bennett, Canadian Prime Minister from 1930 to 1935; Denton Massey conducting a Bible class; Admiral Richard Byrd, speaking on Antarctica; Billy Graham; Princess Elizabeth — the list goes on and on. Add the entertainers, the rock stars, the sports heroes and the great spectacles, and the reasons behind the legend of Maple Leaf Gardens become evident.

But the man who started it all, the man for whom the Gardens will be an everlasting memorial, will not be here to celebrate the building's fiftieth anniversary in November of 1981. Conn Smythe passed away on November 18, 1980.

One of hockey's most memorable moments: Bill Barilko out-manoeuvres Gerry McNeil of the Canadiens in sudden-death overtime to win the Stanley Cup for Toronto on April 21, 1951.
ALEXANDRA STUDIO

CHAPTER **II**   HOCKEY

"SOMETIMES I WOULD RATHER HAVE PLAYED for the Leafs than be Prime Minister of Canada," Lester Pearson once said, an attitude that is typical of the esteem in which hockey fans have held the Toronto team. Hockey has always been a strong tradition, almost a legend at the Gardens. The story of the Toronto Maple Leafs over their first fifty years cannot be told without also telling the story of their driving force, Conn Smythe.

Smythe was a centreman for University of Toronto hockey teams in the 1920s while he was taking a course in civil engineering. He served overseas in World War I, returned to Toronto, worked first for the city government, then started a sand and gravel business. But he didn't drop out of hockey completely, for he talked a U. of T. team into staying together after graduation, named them the Varsity Grads and coached them to the Allan Cup and to an Olympic gold medal in 1928.

Smythe's exposure to professional hockey started in 1926 as a direct result of his involvement on the amateur level. He was hired by Colonel John Hammond to recruit a new team in New York to play in the NHL, and he ended up doing a fine job, signing the likes of Frank Boucher, the Cook brothers and Ching Johnson for the New York Rangers. But the one that got away proved to be his downfall, at least for a while.

One evening during training camp in Toronto, Smythe and his wife, Irene, decided to take the night off. When they returned to their hotel room, Hammond was on the phone. "Where have you been? We had a chance while you were out to add one of the greatest players in the game, Babe Dye. We lost him to Chicago." According to author Ron McAllister, the Babe was indeed worth going after. He could "score with his back turned. . . . He had a shot like a thunderclap and astounding accuracy. . . . He would snap a two-inch plank with one of his drives."

Hammond fired Smythe for losing Babe Dye, and in Foster Hewitt's words, "Smythe was flat on his back, and few could have blamed him if he had stayed down. But that wasn't his way of fighting. He was determined to convince himself, as well as others, that Hammond had made a big mistake. He told his friends that he would go out and organize another team that would beat the pants off the one he had organized for New York."

In 1927 the Toronto St. Pats, under coach Mike Rodden, placed last in the NHL and financial difficulties created even more problems. "They fired me," Rodden said in 1976, "and things got worse. That's when Smythe got into the picture and started dealing with Charlie Querrie, the manager. The asking price for the St. Pats was $160,000." Smythe had received $10,000 in severance pay from the Rangers, bet his money on a University of Toronto football game against McGill, took his winnings and bet them on a hockey game between the Ottawa Senators and the St. Pats. He won again, thereby establishing a stake to begin negotiations for the team.

Smythe put together a financial team including J. P. Bickell, Hugh Aird, Peter Campbell and himself, bought the St. Pats and changed the team name to the Toronto Maple Leafs on February 14, 1927. In 1927 Babe Ruth hit sixty home runs, Jack Dempsey fought Gene Tunney and the Ottawa Senators with King Clancy won the Stanley Cup. The birth of the Leafs marked yet another important event during that golden year of sport.

Carl Voss was the first player to sign a contract with the Leafs, just hours after the new team officially changed its name. "Gentleman" Joe Primeau and Clarence "Happy" Day were with the first Leaf teams. Irvine "Ace" Bailey anchored the wing, and Red Horner was signed in 1928. Horner's arrival was hailed in a poem from the pen of Ted Reeve in the *Toronto Telegram*:

Our Reginald Horner
Leaped from his corner
Full of ambition and fight
He broke up the clash with a furious dash
While the stockholders shrieked with delight.

With such solid players in the line-up, Smythe began moulding a championship team. Harold "Baldy" Cotton came from Pittsburgh for the 1928-29 season, Lorne Chabot was picked up from the Rangers and Andy Blair was signed. Charlie Conacher came up from the Marlies in 1929, and Frank Selke signed Harvey "Busher" Jackson. When Conacher and Jackson were teamed up with Primeau just before Christmas, 1929, one of the most famous lines in hockey history was born, the immortal "Kid Line." The Leafs were quickly becoming the team to deal with in the NHL, and the city loved it. As Trent Frayne wrote in *The Mad Men of Hockey,* Smythe "made hockey so respectable in Toronto that it was right up there with ballet and opera on the town's social scale."

Opening ceremonies for the Ace Bailey benefit of February 14, 1934, the first annual NHL All Star game.
PRINGLE & BOOTH LIMITED

At a Leaf game on January 8, 1938, the Mayor of Moncton, New Brunswick, presented Moncton native son Gord Drillon with a gold watch.
ALEXANDRA STUDIO

Left to right: Defencemen Red Horner, King Clancy and Hap Day of the first Leaf Stanley Cup team, 1932.
ALEXANDRA STUDIO

Then came the King. Smythe decided that he needed a solid defence-man, and because the Ottawa Senators were feeling the financial pinch of the beginning Depression, King Clancy became available. Smythe didn't have the money to buy Clancy's contract, so he went to the races at Toronto's Woodbine Racetrack and put what money he had on one of his colts, Rare Jewel. The horse was running that day at odds of 100 to 1. Rare Jewel won, and Smythe used his winnings to pick up Clancy for $35,000 and two Toronto players. Clancy signed with the Leafs for $8,500 per year and a $1,500 bonus. It was some of the best money Smythe ever spent, money that came to him in a rare string of winning bets just at the most crucial moments.

The King made a difference. "Before that day they sold booster tickets at half price and such," the late Tommy Nayler, a Gardens' equipment man, remembered in a 1976 interview with journalist Roy MacGregor. "But that ended when Clancy came. What hockey player could be good enough to cost $35,000, people asked. They were anxious to see for themselves, and it paid off. From then on there were no more booster tickets."

Smythe now had the team he needed, but without the proper coach or the proper facilities. He fired himself as coach, because in his own words, "I was no good." He hired Art Duncan to fill the spot, built the Gardens in 1931 and in 1932 the Leafs won their first Stanley Cup. This first Cup win came just five years after the new team was formed. Smythe had indeed made a team that would "beat the pants" off the opposition. In doing so he had also created Maple Leaf Gardens, one of the finest arenas in the world.

As with any new building, there were a number of firsts at the Gardens, and they were concerned with hockey. On opening night, a near-capacity crowd of 13,233 showed up to watch the Leafs lose 2-1 to Chicago. Charlie Conacher scored the first and only goal for the Leafs in the building that night. The first amateur game was played on November 13, 1931, the night after the Leafs game, pitting the National Yacht Club team against the Marlboros. The Nats won 3-2 before a crowd of about 5,000 spectators. Buzz Boll scored the first amateur goal in the building, and he also had the honour of incurring one of the first major penalties, when he pushed Bruce Paul of the Nats into the boards hard enough to send Paul to the hospital with a concussion.

The first junior game in the Gardens was played on November 16, 1931, between the Toronto Canoe Club and the University of Toronto Schools.

In front of 2,000 fans, the Marlies beat Hamilton 6-0 on November 17, 1931, recording their first shutout in the Gardens, and also a rare six-goal game. Bob Davidson, later a Leaf standout scored, as did Arthur Jackson, younger brother of Busher Jackson. Arthur was sixteen at the time and was touted as a future equal to his brother.

The Leafs won their first Gardens' game on November 28, 1931, a 4-3 decision over the Boston Bruins. It was an overtime win, with Day, Jackson and Ace Bailey scoring during the regular game, and Horner scoring at one minute, forty-five seconds of the overtime period. In addition to being the Leafs' first Gardens win, it was also their first victory of the season. They had played five games by this time, beating Boston and tying two. The Leafs were in fourth and last place in the international section of the NHL behind the Montreal Maroons, the New York Americans and the Montreal Canadiens.

The fastest goal after the opening face-off was scored by the legendary Charlie Conacher, only seven seconds after the start of a game played on February 6, 1932. According to a newspaper report, "From the face-off the puck was deflected over to the left wing, Busher Jackson picked it up and fed a long pass to Conacher, who blistered a slap shot from the blue line at Boston goalkeeper Wilf Cude." Conacher was to break his left hand the following night during a game against the Detroit Falcons.

Another record was set on April 3, 1933. At 8:30 p.m., the Leafs and the Boston Bruins faced off for the final game to decide the championship of the 1932-33 season. The teams were very evenly matched, and the game didn't end until 1:55 a.m., an overtime record. It was finally won by Toronto when Andy Blair stole an attempted forward pass from Eddie Shore inside the Boston defence area and whipped a pass to Ken Doraty, who scored the only goal of the game.

The 1930s were years of ups and downs for the Leafs. Although they didn't win another Stanley Cup in that decade, they finished first in their division four times, and Ace Bailey became the first Leaf to win a scoring title. Bailey's hockey career was short-lived, however, for on December 12, 1933, he took a body check from the Bruins' Eddie Shore that ended his playing days. Elmer Ferguson of the *Montreal Star* reported, "Bailey was as near death as it was possible for any man to be without passing over the borderline." Both Conacher and Jackson continued the Bailey tradition, though, by winning scoring titles in the 1930s. By the time Babe Dye, the player over whom Hammond had fired Smythe in 1926, finally came to the Leafs, the team was solid as well as spectacular.

But the 1930s marked the end of an era for the Leafs. The great Primeau, Clancy and George Hainsworth all retired in 1936. Hap Day was sold to the New York Americans in 1937, and Conacher and Jackson went to the same team in the 1938-39 season. Charlie Conacher returned to the Gardens in November, 1939, for the first time since he was traded to the Americans. Instead of the cheers he had known for years, he was greeted with cat-calls from Toronto fans. He reacted by raising his hands like a boxer, cheerfully acknowledging the reception.

LEFT: *Right-winger Charlie Conacher, who scored the first Leaf goal in the Gardens, was nominated five times for the NHL All Star team.*

RIGHT: *Centre Syl Apps joined the Leafs during the 1936-37 season and was the first winner of the Frank Calder Trophy for rookie of the year.*
ALEXANDRA STUDIO

Left to right: Trainer Tim Daly, Conn Smythe and publicity director Frank Selke, Sr., prepare to leave for training camp in the 1930s.
ALEXANDRA STUDIO

The world-famous Dionne quintuplets photographed in Leaf sweaters in the 1930s.
REPRINTED WITH PERMISSION FROM THE TORONTO STAR

Yet while these hockey immortals were leaving room on the bench, other names began appearing on the score sheet. Walter "Turk" Broda replaced Hainsworth, Gord Drillon made the All Star Team for the first time in 1938, and Dave "Sweeney" Schriner came to the Leafs from the Americans in 1940. The Leafs were rebuilding for another Stanley Cup, and if anyone led the team during the 1940s, it was Syl Apps.

Smythe had heard reports of Apps' ability, but he figured that anyone with such a name couldn't be a hockey player. Smythe quickly changed his mind when he saw Apps playing football for McMaster University and added the strange name to the Leafs' negotiation list. Apps joined the Leafs in 1936, won the Calder Trophy in 1937 and was selected for the All Star Team the following year. Jack Adams of Detroit said that Apps was a better player than Howie Morenz at the same age, and it wasn't long before Apps began paying dividends to the team and to the Gardens.

The Maple Leafs won their second Stanley Cup in 1942, ten years after their first victory. They staged a dramatic comeback against Detroit after being down three games to one in the final series. Publicity Director Ed Fitkin put it this way, writing in a 1964 Gardens' programme, "The night the Leafs climaxed their tremendous comeback was Saturday, April 18, 1942, a night to remember indeed. . . . Every player was a hero, but the man the fans clamoured for was Syl Apps, the man they all regarded as the heart of the Leafs. He epitomized the old college try. . . . That night, long after the jubilant Leafs had won the game and the Cup, and the joyous dressing room celebration had petered out, Syl headed for his car in the parking lot across from the Gardens. Unknown to him, hundreds of fans had waited all that time for him to appear, and when he did, they virtually mobbed him. He signed autographs until his arm almost fell off, and it was a good hour later before he finally got away."

Syl Apps retired in 1948. Perhaps the best and most fitting reaction came from the *Hamilton Spectator:* "There is only one Apps; there never was another; there never could be. . . . There have been many remarkable athletes in Canadian sport, but few have been more out-standing."

The 1940s and early 1950s were glory years for the Leafs; the Stanley Cup came to the Gardens in 1942, 1945, 1947, 1948, 1949 and 1951. The rosters of these years contained such famous names as Turk Broda, Gaye Stewart, Lorne Carr, Ted Kennedy, Howie Meeker, Walter "Babe" Pratt, Harry Watson, Bob Goldham, Sid Smith, Max Bentley and Cal Gardner. And while writer Jack Batten saw the 1945 team as "Perhaps the most rag-tag, free-form, gutsy team ever to win the Cup," it was the Leafs' farm team that ensured success. "We used to have a great farm system," Tommy Nayler recalled in 1976. "Used to have good

Priceless mementos. Autographs of the 1934-35 Leaf hockey team.

THE GARDENS EXECUTIVE

FORMER MAPLE LEAF HOCKEY PLAYERS NOW ON ACTIVE SERVICE

CONN SMYTHE
MAJOR CONN SMYTHE, M.C.
ON LEAVE
O.C. 30th I.A.A. BATTERY, R.C.A.-A

J. Y. MURDOCH
VICE-PRES.

Major E. W. Bickle, V.D.
PRESIDENT

J. P. BICKELL
CHAIRMAN OF THE BOARD

W. A. H. MacBRIEN
LIEUT.-GEN.
VICE-PRES.

G. R. COTTRELLE

NICK KNOTT
ARMY

WALLY STANOWSKI
R.C.A.F.

NICK METZ
ARMY

JACK FOX, PRINCESS PATS. THE FIRST PRO HOCKEY PLAYER TO MAKE THE SUPREME SACRIFICE IN THE PRESENT WAR.

BOB GOLDHAM
R.C.N.V.

BINGO KAMPMAN
ARMY

BUDDY HELLYER
R.C.A.F.

PETE LANGELLE
R.C.A.F.

JOHNNY McCREEDY
R.C.A.F.

ERNIE DICKENS
R.C.A.F.

FRANK EDDOLS
R.C.A.F.

VICTOR GRIGG
ARMY

THE 30TH SPORTSMENS BATTERY. IN REVIEW AT THE TORONTO ARMOURIES WHERE THEY WERE INSPECTED BY COL. F. F. ARNOLDI D. S. O. IN JUNE, 1942.

PRESIDENT P. J. MULQUEEN OF THE SPORTSMENS PATRIOTIC ASSOCIATION PRESENTING A CHEQUE TO MAJOR CONN SMYTHE O. C. OF THE 30TH BATTERY, WHILE O. H. A. PRES. ROSS CLEMENS AND SECTY. W. A. HEWITT SMILE APPROVAL.

DON METZ
ARMY

ABOVE: *Members of the Leafs' organization made a significant contribution to the war effort, not only through Conn Smythe's 30th Sportsmen's Battery, but also in other branches of the service.*

LEFT: *Leaf captain Syl Apps and Conn Smythe with the Stanley Cup in 1942, presented by League president, Frank Calder.*
ALEXANDRA STUDIO

RIGHT: *Vezina Trophy winner and All Star goalie Turk Broda battled with the scales throughout the late 1940s.*
ALEXANDRA STUDIO

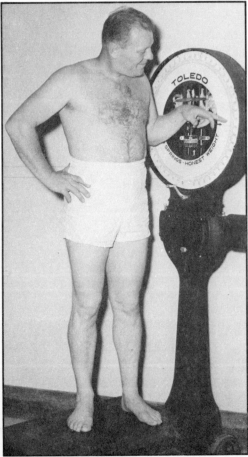

depth. There was a time — 1949, I think — when you could have a guy like Sid Smith come up from the farm club and win the Stanley Cup almost by himself, and then next season was sent back down... because he couldn't make the team."

The string of Stanley Cups ended in 1951. The playoffs that year saw some of the best hockey ever played. The final game in the final series, Leafs versus Canadiens, was a classic. The Leafs' Bill Barilko took the puck, and as Stan Fischler wrote in *Power Play,* "Literally running on the tips of his skates, Barilko lurched over the blueline and in one motion hurled his 5'11", 185-pound body at the puck.... As he stroked the puck from his left, Barilko momentarily floated through the air, his legs spread out behind him, his hands still clutching the stick.... He was still aloft when the puck cleared McNeil's [Gerry, the Canadiens goalie's] raised right glove." It was one of the greatest hockey games ever played, and one of the greatest moments for Leaf supporters in the traditional Toronto-Montreal rivalry.

Unfortunately, Barilko was to die in an airplane accident that summer, and the Leafs weren't to bring another Cup to the Gardens until 1962. This was the beginning of the Imlach era, and the team was to repeat its performance in 1963, 1964 and 1967, the last Cup win to date. In 1959 Punch Imlach said, "I felt that somebody had to believe in those guys, and keep saying so, day and night, until they started believing in themselves. They did." Imlach inherited a team hungry for a Stanley Cup, and on his way to winning he traded a few players and brought up a few more. One of his greatest finds was Dave Keon. "We weren't counting on him at all," Imlach later remembered. "He'd been a good junior, but in a pro tryout at Sudbury hadn't been impressive."

Keon, however, clicked in the majors. He teamed up with the likes of Johnny Bower, Carl Brewer, Tim Horton, Red Kelly and Frank Mahovlich to bring home the silverware four times in six years. But in 1968, the team finished out of the playoffs. The following year it lost the quarter-final, and on April 6, 1969, Imlach was gone, fired by Stafford Smythe. Johnny Bower quit hockey the next day. "I owe too much to Punch," he said, "and I have now played my last game as a Leaf." In the words of Stafford Smythe, "This is the end of the Imlach era. He's all through. Punch brought us back from oblivion, but we have no farm system any more.... We need more young Turks."

Ten years later, Imlach returned as General Manager. The Leafs had already celebrated their fiftieth anniversary, Staff Smythe had passed away in 1971, Harold Ballard was running the team and as the Gardens approached its half-century Imlach was again asked to bring the team back from oblivion.

The Leafs were the main attraction on the ice rink, but there were many other hockey games played at the Gardens, from public school tournaments to international series. The Russians began coming to

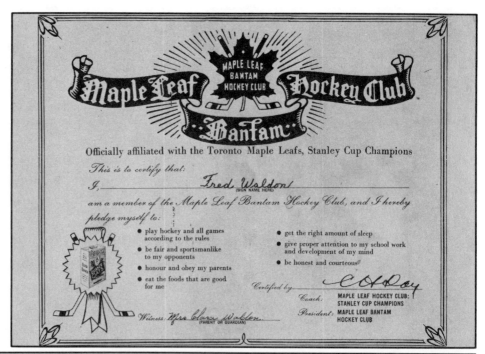

Thousands of Canadian boys joined the Maple Leaf Bantam Hockey Club in the 30s and 40s.

Amateur hockey attracted large crowds during the war. Boston's famed "Kraut Line," pictured here, was a popular fixture on the Ottawa RCAF Flyers team.

The Marlboros won the Allan Cup during their only year of senior competition, 1950-51. Celebrating the win are Stafford Smythe (second from left), captain Bob Pulford, coach Turk Broda (centre) and team director Harold Ballard (second from right).
ALEXANDRA STUDIO

Right-winger Andy Bathgate, a former New York Ranger, helped the Leafs win a Stanley Cup in 1963-64.

the building in the 1950s, and fans can still remember Bobby Orr and Jim McKenny leading the Canadian junior teams against the Russians in the days when Canada used to win international games.

But at that time Canadians had little interest in international hockey, as Sid Smith, former Leaf great, recalls of the first time a Russian team came to North America. On November 22, 1957, the Whitby Dunlops played the Russians. The Soviets scored two quick goals, and then the Canadian team came back to score seven. It was an historic night, and Smith remembers that, "the Russians used white tape on their sticks, which people thought was funny back then." The Russians soon became anything but funny.

In late December, 1969, and early January, 1970, exhibition games were staged at the Gardens with the Russians and Czechs in preparation for the 1970 world hockey championships. By this time the Soviets were becoming a force to be reckoned with in international play. The Canadian team included such future pros as Ken Dryden, Wayne Stephenson and Reg Leach, and such international players as Terry O'Malley, Fran Huck, Brian Conacher and Morris Mott. Names on the Czech roster were becoming known in Canada: Vladimir Dzurila, Ivan Hlinka and future Detroit Red Wing, Vaclav Nedomansky. For the Russians, in those days before the great Canada-Russia series and Canada Cup games, names that still ring a bell are: Vladislav Tretiak, Alexander Ragulin, Alexander Maltsev, Vladimir Mikhailov and Valery Kharlamov. The Russian team was coached by Anatoli Tarasov, a man who made it to the Hockey Hall of Fame.

The best-remembered international game played at the Gardens took place on September 4, 1972. Team Canada rebounded from a 7-3 defeat in Montreal to beat the Soviets 4-1 during the first Canada-Russia series. Phil Esposito, Yvan Cournoyer, Peter Mahovlich and Frank Mahovlich scored for Canada. According to Harold Ballard, this was the series in which people thought "we should win every game." The second game of the 1974 Summit Series was also played at the Gardens, and again Canada beat the Russians 4-1, this time on goals from Ralph Backstrom, André Lacroix, Bobby Hull and J.-C. Tremblay. In 1976, several games in the Super Series were played at the Gardens. Canada and Czechoslovakia played the first game of the finals in the building, and Canada took it 6-0. Later, the series was won in Montreal by a 5-4 score on an overtime goal by Darryl Sittler. These are the highlights of international hockey at the Gardens. A comprehensive list is included in the Chronology.

The Toronto Marlboros have been tenants at the Gardens as long as the Leafs. In fact, as a team the Marlies got their start earlier, in 1926 as opposed to 1927. Although the Marlboros have won the Memorial Cup seven times, like their professional counterparts they lost their first game on Gardens' ice, a 3-2 defeat at the hands of the Toronto Nationals. Both these teams played in the Ontario Hockey Association

Hockey writer, Margaret Scott, talks to a group of "her boys." Left to right: Bill Harris, Frank Mahovlich, Red Kelly, George Armstrong and Dick Duff, during a practice in the 1960s.
ALEXANDRA STUDIO

The dressing room banner reads "Defeat Does Not Rest Lightly on their Shoulders." There were more victories than defeats for the Leafs in 1963, when Kent Douglas, Allan Stanley, Bob Nevin, Carl Brewer, Red Kelly, Tim Horton, Don Simmons and Johnny Bower posed for this photo.

In 1961, defenceman Red Kelly won the Lady Byng Memorial Cup, goalie Johnny Bower, the Vezina Trophy, and rookie-of-the-year, centre Dave Keon, the Calder Memorial Trophy.
JOHN MAIOLA

A smiling George Armstrong (centre) signs autographs during a practice open to the public. These practices annually attract more than 16,000 spectators and autograph hunters, and proceeds are donated to charity.
GRAPHIC ARTISTS

Punch Imlach took over as General Manager of the Leafs in 1979 for a second time. Here, Imlach is interviewed by Cathy Renwald of CHCH-TV at the press reception to announce his return.

Leaf captain Darryl Sittler and Harold Ballard agree to disagree after Sittler had relinquished his position as captain of the team in 1980.

Mike Palmateer in action on Gardens' ice, 1979.
ROBERT SHAVER

Gone but not forgotten: right wing Lanny McDonald ended up with Colorado and left wing Dave Williams (22) with Vancouver in trades designed to bring the Stanley Cup back to the Gardens.

(OHA) then, and one early Marlie graduate was Charlie Conacher. The Marlies and the Senior Marlboros, who won the Allan Cup in 1950, were at one time under Harold Ballard's tutelage; he guided these junior and amateur teams from the 1920s to the 1950s.

It was Ballard who had asked Winston Churchill for permission to use the name Marlborough (both spellings have been used) in 1926, and in 1975 the then Duke of Marlborough wrote Ballard congratulating him on the Marlies' Memorial Cup win. Both during and after Ballard's time, a large number of players have gone up to the Leafs. Even in the last few years a very small list of Marlie graduates would make an impressive team: Carl Brewer, Bob Nevin, Brad Park, Steve Shutt, Mike Palmateer, Bob Dailey, Mark Napier, Mark Howe and over ninety more who are still in professional hockey.

Not all hockey at the Gardens has been professional or near-professional. School hockey was first played there in 1931 between Toronto Canoe Club and University of Toronto Schools, and Harry Neale of TCC recorded the first shutout on this level.

Many levels of hockey and many of the game's most important events have occurred on Gardens' ice. International series, the Allan Cup and Memorial Cup finals, NHL All Star games, Olympic exhibition games, Stanley Cup finals — all were played there at one time or another. Conn Smythe may not have known it, but when he built his ice palace in 1931 to better accommodate the Leafs, he also provided excellent facilities for the young and rising stars of future professional teams.

*A packed house for wrestling in
the 1950s.*

CHAPTER III   WRESTLING AND BOXING

AFTER HOCKEY, WRESTLING has been the most consistently followed sport at Maple Leaf Gardens. From 1931 to 1981 — right from the very first month that the building opened — wrestling events have been regularly scheduled. And right from the beginning Frank Tunney has been associated with the sport.

Tunney is one of the few remaining figures from the earliest days of the Gardens. On November 19, 1931, his Queensbury Athletic Club staged its first wrestling card in the building, with Jim Londos taking on Gino Garibaldi. This bout drew the largest crowd ever to see an indoor sporting event up to that time; over 15,000 people jammed in.

The match lasted one hour, fifteen minutes and seventeen seconds. Londos pinned Garibaldi for the first fall, and after a ten-minute rest period Garibaldi wanted to resume the contest for a second fall. However, Ontario Athletic Commission doctors felt that Garibaldi had had enough, and they didn't allow him to continue. Londos won, reputedly because of the effective use of his "aeroplane whirl" and body slam.

Promoted by Jack Corcoran in association with Frank Tunney, the match was a huge success, and the gross gate was $13,000. George Zaharias, husband of the famous golfer Babe, was also on the card. He defeated Paul Harper during an evening of wrestling where ladies were charged a special rate of twenty-five cents to encourage them to come to the "fights."

Tunney has promoted nearly 2,000 bouts at the Gardens, at first with Corcoran and Deacon Allen, then on his own. There have been many favourites in his stable: Tiger Jeet Singh (the Sadistic Sikh), George Zaharias, Yukon Eric (who panned gold in the ring), Killer Kowalski (the Polish Prince), Pat Flanagan (Ye Olde Irish Wrestler), The Masked Marvel (who is he?), Gorgeous George (one more robe) and Lou Thesz (the Prez of Wrestling). A proper list should also include the scowling Bulldog Brower, the snarling Sheik, the aristocratic Lord Athol Layton, the dignified champion Whipper Billy Watson, Andre the Giant and Haystack Calhoun. But if you ask Frank Tunney which is his greatest card, he replies, "That's easy; my next wrestling bout."

The Angel, a popular Gardens'
wrestler in the 1940s, with Canadian
writers (left to right) Ralph Allen,
Johnny Fitzgerald, Joe Perlove and
Hal Walker, and (standing at
right), a young Frank Tunney.
ALEXANDRA STUDIO

Wrestling greats of the early 1930s,
as they appeared in the first
Gardens' programme.

The genius of a good wrestling promoter like Tunney is to get either
a superlative wrestler with charisma, or one that the crowd loves to
hate. The favourites have to return as well. After the first card filled the
Gardens in 1931, Tunney brought Zaharias back on December 21, 1933,
to wrestle Jim Browning. Londos returned on January 11, 1934, to
fight Rudy Dusek. Then Garibaldi wrestled Dusek later in 1934, affording the fans the opportunity to have a good look at all of them.

Even competing groups, like the Shamrock Athletic Club, didn't
detract from the popularity of Tunney's Queensbury matches. When
the Shamrock Club had Zaharias on the card, Tunney retaliated with
Garibaldi against Dusek. A second competitor, the Maple Leaf Athletic
Club, brought in Vic Christie to wrestle The Masked Marvel on June 9,
1938, as an answer to both other clubs. Tunney was using the tactics of
the Ford Motor Company in his relations with other promoters, pitting Lincolns against Thunderbirds, but all owned by Ford. It was all
good for wrestling at the Gardens, and all good for Tunney.

The first world title match in the building was held on February 16,
1939, with Jim Londos, now a familiar name at the Gardens, battling
Joe Savoldi. Before 5,500 spectators, Londos whipped his rival by pinning him with a body slam after one hour, sixteen minutes and ten
seconds had elapsed. Savoldi figured that Londos had made illegal use
of the ropes in pinning him, and in protest he decided to sit in the
middle of the ring and not move until Londos resumed the fight. No
one bothered with him, though, and Savoldi was still there all alone
when maintenance workers arrived to put in the ice for an upcoming
hockey game. The staff lowered the movable arc lamps from above the
ring, and this finally drove Savoldi into the dressing room. Because of

A Group of World-Famous Wrestling Stars

Gino Garibaldi

Geo. Zaharias

Ray Steele

Jim Londos

Earl Mc Ready

Pat O Shocker

Jim McMillen

See these men in action at the "Gardens"

Lord Athol Layton in the 1960s with Gardens' ushers.
MICHAEL BURNS

BELOW LEFT: *Friends away from the ring, Lord Athol Layton puts the squeeze on Whipper Billy Watson.*

BELOW RIGHT: *An early 1950s bout: Whipper Billy Watson puts a hammerlock on Lou Thesz.*
ALEXANDRA STUDIO

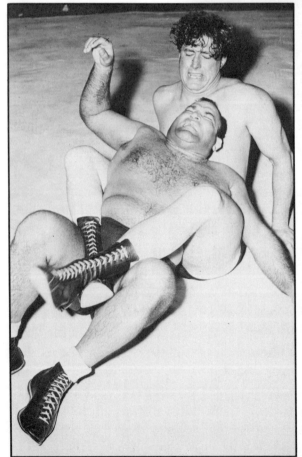

Bulldog Brower, who appeared on wrestling cards throughout the 1960s, hams it up for the camera.

Tag-team matches were popular at the Gardens during the 1950s and 1960s. Pictured here are the Crusaders, Dewey Robertson and Billy "Red" Lyons.

his sit-down strike, the newspapers nicknamed him CIO (Congress of Industrial Organization) thereafter.

According to sports writer Al Stewart, "Every sport has a particular personality, the mere name of whom conjures up in the mind's eye that sport, and all it stands for. Babe Ruth is synonymous with baseball. Rocket Richard means hockey. Stanley Matthews spells out soccer. And Whipper Billy Watson symbolizes the great sport of wrestling."

In the Gardens at least, Watson's name certainly is symbolic of wrestling. His first match there was against Jack Russell on January 10, 1941. Sharing the card that night with the popular Wild Bill Longson, the Whipper defeated his South African opponent. This was a preliminary bout, and it only took Watson twelve minutes and fifty-two seconds to win with a body slam and an arm hold. His clean, scientific style won favour with the audience. "Watson looked very good when on the attack," the *Globe and Mail* reported, "although at the start it looked as if the only way he could beat Russell was by turning out the lights and hitting him with a club."

After this first bout, Watson wrestled many times at the Gardens. One of the highlights was his victory against Earl McCready later in 1941. This was an important win, because McCready, now in the Saskatchewan Sports Hall of Fame, was a top Canadian wrestler at the time, and the match was a definite milestone in Watson's quest for a goal that would become reality some six years later, a chance at the world title.

There were many epic battles at the Gardens during the war years, especially when Frank Tunney designated special matches on behalf of the war effort. Jersey Joe Walcott and Jack Dempsey could be found in the ring as referees. The Angel fought both Watson and The Strangler in 1942 in two extremely brutal matches, and Primo Carnera, a former boxer, went up against Karl "Krippler" Davis in 1946.

On May 15, 1947, Whipper Billy Watson faced Lou Thesz at the Gardens for the World Heavyweight Wrestling Championship. Earlier that year in Indiana, Thesz had won the title from Wild Bill Longson, and he wasn't prepared to relinquish it quickly. In one of the most rugged matches ever seen in Toronto, Watson and Thesz wrestled to a draw in front of 11,000 fans, a result that allowed Thesz to keep the title.

Nevertheless, there was some question about the impartiality of the referee. The fans were for Watson all the way, but "the civic-pride oozing figure was the referee, who all but fell on the back of his head (which would have been a sterling idea) trying to show Thesz that this city treats its visitors with respect." This quote comes from a contemporary *Globe* account that went on to say, "On a number of times that Thesz was lying outside of the ropes, the referee stopped the count at 'eight,' and that seemed to be as far as he wanted to go. After fifty minutes, the referee raised the hands of both fighters to signify a draw,

A Group of Boxing Champions

Tony Canzoneri

Mickey Walker

Maxie Rosenbloom

Max Schmelling

Frank Genaro

Midget Wolgast

Bat Battalino

CANZONERI, Light and Junior Welterweight.   WALKER, Middleweight.
ROSENBLOOM, Light Heavy.   SCHMELLING, Heavyweight.
GENARO, Flyweight.   WOLGAST, Flyweight.   BATTALINO, Featherweight.

and made his exit." Spectators clustered along the aisle threw themselves at the referee *en masse,* and "one woman came at him from well back with a fine rush to jab at him with a hat pin." There were few in the crowd who hoped she didn't succeed.

A rematch was held on February 19, 1948, and again Watson seemed to get the short end of the stick. Thesz threw him out of the ring at one point, the Whipper was counted out and lost the match. He hadn't been able to return to the ring, because wrestler Nanjo Singh, the Cobra, who wasn't even on the card, lit into him with feet and fists. A few of the 8,000 spectators in turn lit into Singh and gave him a good going over before he escaped into the ring. Singh had to have a police escort to leave the building.

Singh and Watson had crossed paths before. They fought in 1942 for the British Empire title, which Watson won, and then again in April, 1945, when Singh took the title. Singh used the "Cobra Hold," which he had developed himself, but which some wrestlers and referees thought was illegal because it choked the opponent. But his victory over the Whipper stood up, at least until their next meeting, when Watson made short work of the Cobra. This last defeat had no doubt fired Singh up enough to attack Watson when Thesz threw him out of the ring.

Watson held the British Empire Championship from 1944 until he retired, losing it three times but regaining it, and he was also two-time winner of the world title.

Watson formed the Whipper Safety Club after a bout at the Gardens resulted in a tragic accident. Leaving the arena, Watson was mobbed by fans seeking autographs. In the push and shove, a youngster was knocked off the curb and killed by an oncoming car. He has always been interested in the welfare of children, and he has been closely associated with the Ontario Society for Crippled Children, an alliance he maintains to this day. He has staged money-raising events, such as snowmobile rallies in aid of the Society, and Harold Ballard has helped out by donating the Gardens for the annual Whipper Watson skate for Timmy.

Because of his four-decade involvement in wrestling at the Gardens, and because of his humanitarian work, he was honoured at an Appreciation Night held in the building on December 17, 1978. The card for the evening featured some of the best: Rick "Nature Boy" Flair, Ricky Steamboat, Gene Kiniski and Dino Bravo. It was a thrilling and appropriate way to pay tribute to a champion. Recognizing his contributions to the sport and to Canadian life, the Canadian government later awarded him the Order of Canada.

Athletes who had a first sport other than wrestling were in vogue during the early 1950s, including Doug Hepburn, a former weightlifter, and Gene Kiniski, a football player. About this time tag-team matches began to gain prominence, as did Lord Athol Layton; he began to captivate Gardens' crowds as a headliner on February 8, 1951. Layton had one of the most splendid physiques in the sport, and when he was matched against Watson it was a sight to behold. In response to the charge that the sport is a fake, Frank Tunney merely glances over the card featuring some of these names and says, "Go into the ring with them."

A final note is necessary concerning world title matches held in the Gardens. Of the four such events staged in Toronto, two occurred at the Gardens. On January 24, 1963, Lou Thesz defeated Buddy Rogers in the building to gain his seventh world title. Thesz had previously wrestled for the title eleven times since 1937, winning six times and losing five. In three title bouts with Watson, Thesz was able to win two, but he was to lose it again in 1966 to Gene Kiniski, the last time he was to fight for the crown. The second Gardens' world title match happened in 1977 when Harley Race beat Terry Funk.

Over the years there has been as much exciting wrestling under the Gardens' roof as anyone could ask for. The dominant figures have

ABOVE: *Canadian actor Lorne Greene watches a match with promoter Frank Tunney in the 1960s.* ALEXANDRA STUDIO

LEFT: *Canadian fighter Charlie Belanger as portrayed by Lou Skuce. A Gardens' favourite, Belanger was Canada's White Hope Champion in the early 1930s.*

RIGHT: *Amateur boxing was popular at the Gardens during the 1940s. Here, Denton Massey (speaker) appears with fight promoters Jack Dempsey and Frank Tunney (to Massey's left), introducing two young boxers at an awards ceremony in 1945.*

INSET: *Frank Tunney (right) with one of his many great fighters, Lil' Arthur King. King and Dave Castilloux fought more bouts at the Gardens than any other fighters.* MICHAEL BURNS

been Tunney and Watson. Because of them, the sport of wrestling has gained a large following in the city, many young wrestlers have been able to test their skills in the ring, and some of the world's best have appeared before the Toronto fans.

There have been many wrestling matches at the Gardens, but the ring has been set up almost as frequently for boxing. Next to hockey and wrestling, there have been more boxing events than anything else, and more world championships in all categories have been held than for any other sport. Many fighters and promoters have contributed to the sport under the lights of Maple Leaf Gardens, and are now familiar names: Deacon Allen, Frank Tunney, Harold Ballard, Irv Ungerman, Jack Dempsey, Muhammad Ali, George Chuvalo, Clyde Gray, Sammy Luftspring and Joe Louis, to name but a few of the most famous.

The first true boxing night at the Gardens was a championship programme organized by the Lions Club on May 2, 1932. It was said at the time that this was one of the finest amateur championships ever staged in the city, and the bouts attracted one of the largest crowds ever to attend an amateur event in Toronto. The contestants fought for

interprovincial championships, and Montreal boxers ended up winning five of the seven bouts. Three other, non-interprovincial contests were held, inter-city events in which Horace "Lefty" Gwynne outpointed Jackie Callura, Morrie Bomile won a decision over Joe Abramowitz and Ted Phillips beat Cliff Rhamey of the Prince Athletic Club. The card was concluded with two wrestling matches. A feature of the evening was the presentation of a gift of appreciation to Lou Marsh, who had officiated during this night and in Lions Club matches for the previous ten years.

This success was quickly followed, on May 12 and 13, by an Olympic exhibition series to prepare Canadian boxers for the Los Angeles Games to be held that July. Yet another amateur bout was held on May 16 of the same year when W. L. "Young" Stribling from Macon, Georgia, defeated Joe Doctor in the ninth round. Doctor was disqualified for "not trying."

The first professional fight in the building came just three nights later, on May 19, 1932. "Panama" Al Brown of Colon, Panama, fought Emile "Spider" Pladner of Paris, France. This main bout of the evening was refereed by Lou Marsh, but his duties were light, because Brown knocked out Pladner in less than two minutes.

Also on this card was Lefty Browne, featherweight Olympic champion for 1932, who was making his professional debut. He defeated Tommy Andrews of Buffalo in the first round. Wee Willie Davis of Pennsylvania fought Bobby Leitham of Montreal. In the final match on the card, Eddie Judge of Toronto opposed Vince Glionna, also a Toronto fighter.

The Dominion Boxing Championships were held in the building on May 21-22, 1934. It was a disappointing event, and during the thirteen bouts there seemed little to choose from among the fighters. There were six split decisions, one knockout, one technical knockout and one disqualification. A losing contestant in the 135-pound class was Sammy Luftspring, a fighter who would later make quite a name for himself at the Gardens. The press was not happy about the loss. According to the *Globe and Mail,* "It must have been George Bland's birthday. Not only was he awarded an apparently lucky split decision over Sammy Luftspring, but the judges must have watched him with one eye shut when they gave him the decision over Harvey Fleet in a semi-final bout."

The first great name in boxing to appear at the Gardens was The Brown Bomber, Joe Louis of Detroit. He appeared in an exhibition on November 13, 1935, sparring four rounds with each of four opponents. Louis beat them all handily, and it was apparent that each one preferred moving as far away as possible, to closing with him. Louis' display was preliminary to the main event, where Freddy Miller, Featherweight Champion of the World, outpointed Roger Bernard. Many fans were more interested in Louis, however, and his awesome performance

George Chuvalo with his manager,
Irv Ungerman (centre), and trainer
Ted McWhirter during the 1973
World Championship fight with
Muhammad Ali.

An autographed picture of the fight
that many think was the greatest
bout ever held in the Gardens.
REPRINTED WITH PERMISSION FROM
THE TORONTO STAR

reinforced the opinions of those who expected The Brown Bomber to be the next Heavyweight Champion of the World.

On February 19, 1936, the largest crowd in the history of boxing up to that time packed into the Gardens to watch Red Munroe be crowned the White Hope Champion of Canada and thereby qualify for the Jack Dempsey elimination tournament to be held in New York City. Munroe defeated four opponents to win a purse of $500 and a trophy, which was presented by Mayor Sam McBride. The capacity crowd encouraged one Toronto columnist to write, "It goes to prove once more what an appeal a sport novelty has to the public, and although there was a lot of action, Joe Louis will still be safe."

Frank Tunney's Queensbury Club sponsored yet another White Hope Tournament on April 22, 1936. The newspapers took a dim view of the proceedings, though, and one was led to comment that there wasn't "a white hope in the car load." The Brown Bomber was still safe.

Later in 1936 the Gardens hosted Olympic boxing trials in preparation for the Berlin Olympics. Sammy Luftspring and several other fighters boycotted the trials in protest against Nazi Germany's anti-semitic policies, attending instead the People's Olympics held in Barcelona, Spain.

A white hope to defeat the triumphant Joe Louis was still very much an issue to boxing fans, and a double tournament was held in the same year. This particular set of matches was sponsored by the Apex Olympic Club. Although Joe Louis continued to reign supreme, Toronto's strong interest in boxing did not diminish.

There were a number of bouts in late 1936 and early 1937, and though it might seem incredible today, Sammy Luftspring had four fights in as many months before meeting Gordon Wallace for the Canadian welterweight title on April 2, 1937. Luftspring lost a split decision before 8,524 spectators. Fighters and fight fans are superstitious, and it was rumoured that the loss may have been the result of bad omens: Luftspring had to have his gloves replaced before the match because the first pair was too tight. It was generally agreed that Luftspring had not been outclassed and a rematch should be arranged.

There was a lot of boxing at the Gardens during 1939. Twelve nights were devoted to the sport, six of which saw Dave Castilloux fight. One of the biggest events of this early war year featured a World Bantamweight Championship match between Georgie Pace and Lou Salica. Pace retained the title by virtue of a draw, and even though attendance may have been affected by poor weather, 8,500 fans contributed to the $10,000 gross gate.

This was a bout where there were two sick fighters who both considered that they had won. According to Salica's manager, "It was close all right, but I thought we had won. . . . Anyway, we're going to

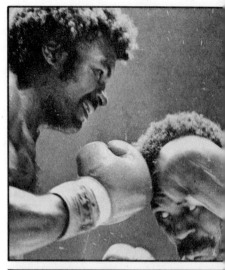

ABOVE: *Canadian Clyde Gray (left) battles José Napoles in a World Welterweight bout on September 22, 1973.*
REPRINTED WITH PERMISSION FROM THE TORONTO STAR

BELOW: *Gray knocks Napoles through the ropes but is unable to win the title.*
TIBOR KOLLEY

claim the title. We have as much right to it now as Pace. . . . Salica just got over a session with pneumonia, and was never quite himself." From the Pace camp: "I thought George won nine rounds and was away off by himself. But George wasn't right. He was sick all week."

Throughout the war and into the 1960s there was plenty of professional action at the Gardens. Familiar names continued to pop up at regular intervals. Dave Castilloux was still fighting in 1948; in about eight years he had been involved in over twenty matches. Lil' Arthur King and Alan McFater were becoming regulars. King started to turn it on in 1946 when he fought in the building six times; he fought nine more times the next year. Three more bouts followed in 1948 before he began running out of opponents; he was winning much more than he was losing, but the calibre of the opposition kept him from making great strides toward international championships. He made a few appearances from 1950 to 1957, but his reign was over at the Gardens, and the spot was filled, at least in total number of matches, by Alan McFater.

McFater first appeared in 1949. Within three weeks of each other he fought two opponents and had the stamina to come back a month later (January 9, 1950) to face Spider Thompson. A tough and resilient fighter, he had four more matches by March 20 winning every one. McFater finished off the year with four more bouts at the Gardens, then eleven more in 1951, and an additional five the next year.

The popularity of the local boxer declined rapidly in about 1953, because the idea of the "Friday Night Fights" was giving way to a desire on the part of the fans to watch the sport's big names compete in championship matches. As well, the advent of closed circuit television radically affected the very nature of fight promotion. As a result of these forces, there was no boxing at all in the building during 1954 and from this year on, live boxing events would be held only sporadically at the Gardens.

However, 1956 was a significant year for Canadian boxing. On June 11 a new face appeared in the Gardens' ring, George Chuvalo, a young man who was later to hold the Canadian heavyweight title and come within a whisker of the world championship. Chuvalo defeated Johnny Arthur in June, beat Howard King in October and was featured in the main event with Bob Hiehler on November 19. It was a busy year. Frank Tunney kept Chuvalo working, pitting him against three opponents in 1957 and four more in 1958. The last bout of 1958 was against James Parker, a boxer of note whom Chuvalo soundly defeated. It was felt at the time that Chuvalo could be developed into a world-class heavyweight, and people were already speaking of him as the next Tommy Burns, the only Canadian to hold the world heavyweight title.

One of Chuvalo's most famous fights occurred on November 17, 1959, when he and Yvon Durelle, the New Brunswick fisherman, stood toe to toe and battled it out until Durelle was finally beaten. Five nights later, George was ready for even tougher competition. This time on the Gardens' giant screen, fans watched Chuvalo lose to Floyd Patterson on closed circuit television. Then live at the Gardens Chuvalo also lost to Ernie Terrell, World Boxing Association champion. Top priced tickets were $5.00.

George Chuvalo finally got his chance at the world title when he met Muhammad Ali at the Gardens on March 29, 1966. Ali was the undefeated Heavyweight Champion of the World at the time. Fight fans had already seen him on the Gardens' giant screen, when he "stung like a bee for the crowd to see" and beat Sonny Liston on May 25, 1965. Another closed circuit broadcast in the building, this one on November 22, 1965, showed Ali defeating Patterson.

Ali was in trouble with the United States Justice Department. He had changed his name from Cassius Clay for religious reasons and also because he felt it was a slave name. Drawing attention to his conversion to Islam and his slave heritage were not the things to do in the mid-1960s. Ali made his position even worse when he said, "I ain't got no trouble with them Viet Congs," and refused to be inducted into the American armed forces. He was sentenced to five years in prison for resisting the draft, a sentence which he never served. He was branded a draft dodger and went from American hero to American undesirable within the space of a year.

Ali was supposed to fight Ernie Terrell, but no arena in the United States would take the bout. Then Harold Ballard stepped in. As Executive Vice-President of the Gardens, Ballard took the responsibility for offering the Gardens as a site for a bout between Ali and George Chuvalo. The offer was accepted, and over 400 reporters from all over the world descended on the building. Press accommodations, according to Jimmy Breslin of the *New York Herald Tribune,* were among the best he had seen anywhere. Prime seats were put on sale for $100 each, the highest ever at the Gardens for any event. Even Howard Cosell came, but he seemed more interested in hockey than in the upcoming fight, asking hockey-related questions such as how Dave Keon was doing.

Ballard had cleared his decision with John Bassett and Staff Smythe, but not everyone was in total accord. Ali's presence at the Gardens so infuriated Conn Smythe that he resigned as Director of the Gardens. In the words of this old patriot and war veteran, staging such a fight was putting "cash ahead of class." Smythe was in Florida when the bout was announced in the media, and he called Ballard to say he would resign if the plan proceeded. He even had Stafford Smythe phone Ballard. "I told them," Ballard said later, "that I didn't give a damn what they did, that I was running the damn place, and that the fight was going on." And the fight did go on.

ALL CANADA SPORTS PROMOTIONS

AND BOBBY ORR ENTERPRISES

PRESENTS THE GREATEST FIGHT CARD IN MANY, MANY YEARS

BRITISH COMMONWEALTH WELTERWEIGHT CHAMPIONSHIP

CLYDE GRAY

EDDIE BLAY

12 ROUNDS

CLYDE GRAY
OF CANADA

vs

EDDIE BLAY
OF GHANA

MAPLE LEAF GARDENS - MONDAY, FEBRUARY 12 -'73

CANADIAN LIGHTHEAVYWEIGHT CHAMPIONSHIP

12 ROUNDS   CHAMPION — WINNIPEG

AL SPARKS

GARY   **vs**   NO. 1 CONTENDER — BRANTFORD

SUMMERHAYS

AL SPARKS — CHAMPION

GARY SUMMERHAYS

3RD BOUT - MIDDLEWEIGHT

GARY BROUGHTON vs BOY McMILLAN

BRANTFORD — NO. 1 CONTENDER   **10 ROUNDS**   TOLEDO, OHIO — FORMER A.A.U. CHAMPION

PLUS AN ADDITIONAL EXCEPTIONAL BOUT

FIRST BOUT AT 8 P.M. SEE IT LIVE!

TICKETS AVAILABLE AT . . .

MAPLE LEAF GARDENS

ROYCE DUPONT POULTRY PACKERS
1526 Dupont Street

TOPS RESTAURANT
317 Yonge Street

AND AT ALL OTHER AGENCIES AND ALL GYMS

PRICES

CLUB CIRCLE	RINGSIDE & REDS	BLUES	GREEN & GRAYS
$15.	$10.	$8.	$5.

(TAX INCLUDED)

When Ali arrived, he went directly to Ballard's office and asked, "Which way is east?" Once shown, he knelt down and prayed towards Mecca. If he was praying for success, he certainly received it on the evening of March 29. It was one of the best fights ever seen at the Gardens, and although Ali won, Chuvalo was still on his feet after fifteen rounds. Not a bad performance for a man Ali had called "an old washer woman" at the press conference.

The match was a boon to Chuvalo's professional career, because he was then able to arrange bouts with George Foreman and Jimmy Ellis, both of which he lost. After re-establishing himself in the United States, Ali returned three times on the Gardens' giant screen, beating Jerry Quarry on October 26, 1970, defeating Oscar Bonavena on December 7, 1970, and losing to Joe Frazier on March 8, 1971. The last fight was staged in New York, but closed circuit television brought it to 15,000 people in the Gardens and an estimated 300 million spectators around the world.

Ali appeared at other times on the giant screen at the Gardens, fighting Bob Foster, Ken Norton and Joe Frazier before regaining the world title through a rematch with Foreman. These fights, and other world-class matches presented at the Gardens via closed circuit television made it obvious that the electronic age was here to stay. The lesser lights in the boxing world would have to remain in the obscurity of gymnasiums and smaller arenas until their turn came to appear before the world, once they were good enough. Gone were the days of the "Friday Night Fights" when local favourites like Sammy Luftspring had a substantial following in Toronto who would jam into the Gardens to cheer him on.

A list of great fights in the building would also have to include the world heavyweight title match of December 4, 1961, when Patterson knocked out McNeeley, Benvenuti's fight on September 17, 1968, against Art Hernandez, Donato Paduano's October 17, 1970, contest against Colin Fraser, or the Canadian-Soviet bouts of August 17, 1975.

There are other fighters who helped establish a boxing tradition at the Gardens and deserve to be mentioned. Like George Chuvalo, Clyde Gray had a number of fights in the building before getting a shot at the world title, this time in the welterweight division. The Gardens held its first Commonwealth Welterweight Championship on February 12, 1973. Staged by Irving Ungerman's All Canada Sports Promotions and Bobby Orr Enterprises, the fight was a thriller. Gray took the title from the current champion, Eddie Blay of Ghana, and qualified for a chance at the world crown.

Gray's opportunity came on September 22, 1973, but he was defeated by World Welterweight Champion José Napoles. This bout was the first in the "Fight a Month" series at the Gardens, otherwise known as "Ali Presents," because it was to be televised internationally with

commentary by Ali and Howard Cosell. Ungerman and Orr also promoted these matches. Besides setting the precedent in world television of a prolonged boxing series, it was also the first time in the history of the sport that subscriptions had been sold for a group of bouts. Although Gray lost to Napoles and ended his hopes for a world title, he fought twice more in 1974 to retain his Commonwealth Championship.

The two biggest fights of 1980, both between Sugar Ray Leonard and Roberto Duran and both broadcast world wide, drew capacity houses to the Gardens. The global television gross was the largest in the history of sport, larger even than for Ali's bouts. The first match, held in Montreal, saw Duran defeat Leonard, while in the rematch staged in New Orleans, Duran lost the title when he stopped fighting in the eighth round.

These are the super events and superstars of the boxing world. When Muhammad Ali retired from boxing, something seemed to go out of the sport even though he fought some very poor bouts, before he left the game, helping neither his reputation nor boxing in general. Duran's questionable conduct in the 1980 rematch against Leonard cast further doubts on the sport. Even though it was announced later in 1980 that Ali would again come out of retirement, the state of boxing today has raised real questions about future matches.

Boxing has been a tradition at the Gardens. Even when interest waned due to giant screen telecasts, the Gardens did its best to keep the live matches going. Although internationally important bouts will doubtless continue to be seen on the giant screen, a wait-and-see attitude will have to be adopted, and the fight fan can only hope that local and Canadian championship matches will again appear in Maple Leaf Gardens.

The six-day bicycle race was a
popular event at the Gardens
during the Depression.
ALEXANDRA STUDIO

CHAPTER IV MORE SPORTS: LACROSSE TO BASKETBALL

IN THE SPORTING WORLD, hockey, wrestling and boxing have always reigned supreme at the Gardens. Still, it has been said that every sport, with the exception of the illegal bull fight, has taken place under the Gardens' roof. This is not quite true; some sports haven't made it into the building, but these are very, very few. Maple Leaf Gardens is a sports palace in the widest sense of the word, hosting at one time or another everything from lacrosse, speed-skating and bicycle races to tennis, water polo and basketball.

After the three major sports, the next game to appear in chronological order was lacrosse. On May 3, 1932, the Maple Leaf lacrosse team squared off against the Tecumsehs, with King Clancy of hockey fame facing off the ball to begin the match. The early popularity of the sport is witnessed by the fact that 8,000 fans showed up for this International Lacrosse League game. Bucko McDonald of the hockey Leafs also played on the lacrosse team, and he scored a goal to help the Toronto club to a 12-5 victory.

The first Mann Cup lacrosse playoffs were held on October 21 of the same year. The Winnipeg Argos, who had earlier beaten the Squamish Indians, lost to the Ontario champions, the Mimico Mountaineers, by a score of 16-6. The Cup game was also held in the building, when on October 24 Mimico defeated Winnipeg 4-2. Both goalies were brilliant; there was no scoring in the first period, an oddity in lacrosse.

Over the years there were a number of other games at the Gardens, and the Mann Cup was contested on several occasions. This Cup is the symbol of senior lacrosse supremacy, but Toronto also had an entry in the Professional Lacrosse League during the 1960s. Lacrosse did not endure in the building, however, because interest in the sport was never as high as it was for hockey.

Tennis has been around the Gardens for years. As far back as April 3, 1933, Bill Tilden brought a touring exhibition to the building, and in 1935 he returned with Wimbledon champion Ellsworth Vines. Tilden was considered one of the best players in the world, but he lost to Vines on this occasion in straight sets, 6-3, 8-6, before 4,500 spectators. To give Vines his due, he was the reigning world professional tennis champion, and had recently won the O'Brien Tennis Tournament. But Tilden was tired, and he showed it. He had arrived only a few hours before the match, driving in from a previous game in Montreal. This was on a Saturday; on the preceding Wednesday he had driven from Rochester to New York City, then to Montreal, and only then to Toronto. These were the exhausting days before easy and rapid plane travel, but Tilden still had enough energy to team up with Vines in a doubles match to beat Hans Neussel and George Lott.

Vines returned to the Gardens on April 26, 1937, to play against another Wimbledon champion, Fred Perry. Perry won a four-set match, even though Vines was "foggin' them in." Over all, though, Vines was still on top by a long way, because Perry had lost twenty-three more matches to Vines during the tour than he had won. As a footnote, Perry again beat Vines at the Wembley Empire Pool in England in 1937; this was a match of great international prestige at the time.

Vines and Perry came back to the Gardens in 1938, but Vines was unbeatable, so the promoters began looking for a new face. They came up with Don Budge, who played in the building on March 11, 1939, along with Vines, A. H. Chapin, Jr. and Dick Skeen. Budge was one of the rare Grand Slam champions of tennis, and he defeated Vines during this match. Part of Budge's fame had to do with the fact that he and Baron von Cramm had played one of the greatest tennis games ever in front of Adolph Hitler.

War interrupted the tour, but before Budge joined the service he and the much older Bill Tilden returned to the Gardens on April 25, 1941. They were accompanied by Alice Marble and Mary Hardwicke, the first women athletes to play any sport in the building.

The opening ceremonies for this match were fitting for wartime. While the band played the national anthems, Mary Hardwicke stood rigidly under a Union Jack at one end of the dimmed arena and Alice Marble stood at attention under the Stars and Stripes at the other. Marble, "who combined feminine allure with masculine play," easily defeated Hardwicke, England's best, 6-0, 6-4, before about 2,000 fans. The outcome was predictable to a degree, because Marble was the number one women's player at the time.

Don Budge teamed up with Hardwicke in mixed doubles to beat Tilden and Marble 2-6, 6-1, 6-2. The reports say that the singles matches weren't very exciting (the men also played each other), but all the contestants seemed to warm up a bit in the doubles.

When Budge returned from the war, he challenged Bobby Riggs, the world tennis champion who is better known today for his match against Billy Jean King. Budge and Riggs played the thirty-first game of their tour at the Gardens on May 1, 1946, in front of 2,200 spectators. Budge won the singles match in straight sets and now trailed Riggs only 15-16 in the aggregate score. In a marathon doubles match,

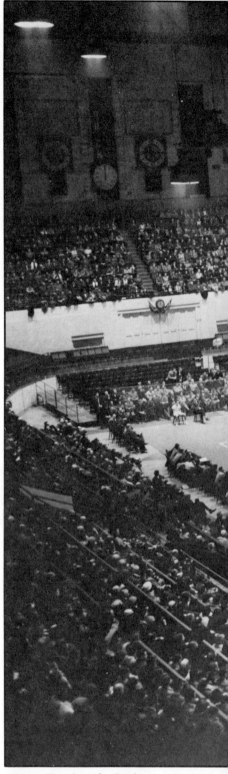

ABOVE: *Tennis at the Gardens in 1961.*
ALEXANDRA STUDIO

LEFT: *Ilie Nastase in the Tennis Challenge match held at the Gardens on April 23, 1980.*

RIGHT: *Jimmy Connors was Nastase's opponent at the 1980 Tennis Challenge.*

The Gardens set up for the Aqua
Parade of 1948.
ALEXANDRA STUDIO

Buster Crabbe, Olympian and actor,
poses with two of his cast from his
Water Follies of 1941.
ALEXANDRA STUDIO

Riggs and Budge took on Johnny Faunce and Wayne Sabin, finally winning 9-7 a mere half-hour before their train was due to depart.

The popularity of tennis in the Gardens continued over the years. Great stars like Jack Kramer, Frank Sedgman, Ken McGregor, Lew Hoad and Pancho Gonzales appeared at various times. Even show business got into the act; on March 30, 1973, a benefit combination musical-tennis exhibition was held featuring Desi Arnaz, Jr. and Liza Minelli. The proceeds went to the Children's Asthma Research Institute and Hospital.

In the tradition of earlier pro tours, a Challenge Tennis match was booked into the Gardens on April 23, 1980, this time between the bad boys of tennis, Jimmy Connors and Ilie Nastase. To watch the game, fans paid between $5.00 and $20.00, or $100 in a special section, and they were rewarded when the boys decided to stir things up a bit. Connors wore a Toronto Maple Leaf sweater, and Nastase donned the colours of the Montreal Canadiens. Both players returned on February 4-8, 1981, for the $500,000 Molson Challenge Tournament, joined by other superstars of tennis: John McEnroe, Bjorn Borg, Vitas Gerulaitis, Wotjek Fibak, Sandy Mayer and Johan Kriek. They attracted the biggest gross in Gardens' history. In an upset victory, Gerulaitis defeated Borg and went on to beat McEnroe in the final, smashing his way to $175,000 in prize money.

Some sports, like tennis, have appeared frequently in the building, while others, like softball, have been played only once. Over 11,000 people turned up on November 9, 1945, to watch Jax of New Orleans, Women's World Softball Champions, take on two local teams. The Jax beat both Simpson's Big Store Sallies and the Sunday Morning Class by scores of 2-1, and all proceeds went to the Hospital for Sick Children.

Aquatics have also had their day at the Gardens. On May 27-31, 1941, Buster Crabbe and his Water Follies glided through 80,000 gallons of water in an "entertaining extravaganza of beauty, brawn, glamour and gaiety." Crabbe was the former Olympic swimming star who portrayed the first Tarzan in the movies. He brought with him the world's largest portable pool, measuring seventy feet long by twenty-five wide and seven feet deep at the diving end. Attendance was only 1,300 the first night, but picked up for the duration of Crabbe's stay. After the show and the removal of the tank, dancing was accompanied by the Coquettes, an all-female orchestra. Crabbe returned in 1942 for the second and last time.

One kind of event that was tremendously popular in North America during the Depression was six-day bicycle racing, not only because interest ran high, but also because indoor arenas provided welcome shelter and warm berths for people out of work for at least as long as the events lasted. The first such race took place in the Gardens on

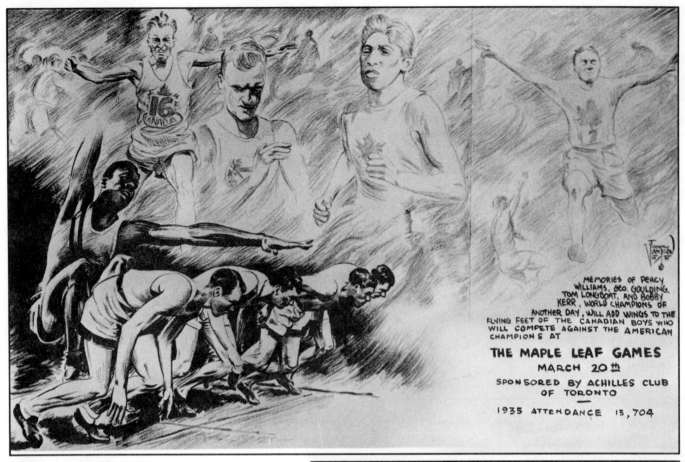

ABOVE: *An advertising poster promoting the 1936 Maple Leaf Games at the Gardens.*

RIGHT: *Jim Ryan of Kansas breaking the tape at an early Gardens' track meet.*
ALEXANDRA STUDIO

OPPOSITE, TOP: *The first track meet at the Gardens, March 22, 1935, was sponsored by the Achilles Club of Toronto.*
ALEXANDRA STUDIO

OPPOSITE, BOTTOM: *Preparing for a track meet in 1976.*
GRAPHIC ARTISTS

Champion high-jumper, Debbie Brill.
GREG LOCKHART

October 21, 1934. The event began at 12:30 on a Sunday afternoon to the crack of a starting gun fired by Premier Mitchell Hepburn. Over the six days, the cyclists travelled 3,045 miles and three laps, with the Maple Leaf team from Toronto staving off a last minute sprint by the British Empire team led by the great champion William J. "Torchy" Peden. The Toronto team had picked up a one-lap lead by 11 p.m., an hour before the end of the race, and they were able to hold on until the finish. The crowd erupted when Willie Spencer announced the winners after this popular victory. The Dutch team placed third, followed by the Germans, the Americans, the Swiss and the French. The Belgian team had dropped out of the gruelling event on the previous afternoon.

Similar races were held in the two following years, with the Americans winning in 1935, after 2,551 miles, and once more in 1936. Although Peden placed fourth in 1935 and second in 1936, these records do not do justice to his overall career. Born in Vancouver, British Columbia, in 1906, Peden was a world-class rider who amassed an incredible total of thirty-nine track championships. This formidable record stood until 1965, when Rick van Steenbergen broke it at the Gardens with a fortieth victory. Peden was on hand to present the trophy, doubtless proud that his mark had stood for so long as a goal for international riders. A great Canadian champion, little-known today, Torchy Peden died in 1980, but not before he had been inducted into the Sports Hall of Fame where his gold-plated track bike hangs as a memorial to him and to his accomplishments.

Interest in six-day races waned in the late 1960s, but with the increased popularity of cycling in the 1980s perhaps similar events will be staged at the Gardens once again.

Where speed was important, another Canadian, Herb Flack of Toronto, made the best of his abilities as a junior skater to win two upset victories over the American senior team in a 1934 speed-skating meet. The entire programme was a great success, and in the words of one newspaper commentator: "I have seen many skating events, both indoor and outdoor, but never has there been a more enthusiastic crowd. The speed-skating events were not tireless parades . . . where skaters put on the pressure in the last two laps only. Every event was a race of speedsters giving their best throughout."

The meet also included figure-skating exhibitions, the first time that both forms of the sport were combined in Toronto. On the second day of the meet, 5,500 people saw Flack take the North American senior skating title by twenty points. This was the only time that speed-skating was held in the building.

The Roller Follies came to the Gardens on May 9, 1942, as the first of a number of roller-skating events. The forerunner of the modern-day Roller Derby, the Follies provided a "snappy" show under the auspices of the Strathcona Club. An audience of 5,000 saw comedy acts, solos and a children's performance of "Mary Had a Little Lamb," certainly a far cry from the rough and tumble of the Roller Derby of the 1960s and 1970s.

March 7, 1971, saw the first Canadian appearance of the Roller Derby. The bill featured the Midwest Pioneers against the San Francisco Bombers, and it was promoted by the mention of "statuesque girls." The star for the Bombers was a Canadian from Montreal, Francine Cochu, who married an American skater, Larry Smith, in 1967. "The two dedicated skaters naturally spent their honeymoon on the Derby's national tour," according to one *Globe and Mail* reporter. Francine was later to appear at the Gardens with the Canadian Chiefs, as the Roller Derby had its brief heyday more than a decade ago.

Track meets have been popular at the Gardens ever since the Telegram-Maple Leaf Games began in 1963. But track events were held there even in the 1930s. Back on March 22, 1935, a meet was held which starred Glenn Cunningham, the famous Kansas miler, and 14,000 fans jammed the building hoping to see him break his Canadian indoor mile record. Cunningham won in four minutes, seventeen point seven seconds (4:17:7), but he failed to undercut the time he had set in Hamilton the week before.

Track didn't return to the Gardens for twenty-five years. Then, on January 25, 1963, the first Maple Leaf-Telegram Indoor Games were staged. The meet was a resounding success, so much so that one meet organizer asked, "What do we do for an encore?" His enthusiasm had to do with the number of records that fell and the number of fans that attended. The British Empire Games in Perth, Australia, had recently concluded. Bruce Kidd, a rising young Canadian star from the University of Toronto, had won a gold medal in the six-mile race, a bronze in the three-mile and represented his country in the twenty-six mile marathon. In the Toronto games, Kidd set a Canadian three-mile mark by lapping the competition and sprinting the last half-mile.

Nor was this the only record to fall. In the first event of the competition, more than 16,000 people watched as Nancy McCredie of Brampton set a Canadian record in the shotput, while in the last event Dave Tork of the United States broke the world indoor record in the pole vault. Tork's mark did not stand for long, though; it was broken in Oregon less than twenty-four hours later.

These athletes were running on a track that had been custom-built for the Gardens at a cost of $25,000. Bill Crothers, making his debut, won the 1,000-yard race, an accomplishment he was to repeat in 1964, 1966 and 1967. He also won the 600-yard race in 1965.

The meet became an annual event, and there have been a number of highlights over the years. In 1964, Kidd successfully defended his three-mile record, and Harry Jones, who held the world record in the fifty-yard hurdles, competed and won his race.

Bob Seagren of the United States was supreme in pole vaulting in 1966, 1967 and 1969. There were several Canadian winners during the 1967 games, including Bill Crothers, Harry Jerome in the fifty-yard dash, Abby Hoffman in the 880-yard event, Dave Bailey in the mile and Dave Ellis in the three-mile event. The three-mile race is worth looking at, for from 1963, when Bruce Kidd first won, to 1968, the winning time dropped by over a minute-and-a-half, from thirteen minutes, thirty-four point six seconds (13:34:6) to twelve minutes, fifteen point two seconds (12:15:2).

Many memorable athletes have competed in the Maple Leaf-Telegram Games. In 1966, Wyomia Tynes of Tennessee State set a world record, and she returned in 1969, along with two other world record stars, Abby Hoffman and Tracy Smith. An Olympic repeat was staged in 1969, when American Olympians Tommie Smith and John Carlos squared off in the 300-yard dash. Smith won in a time of three minutes, fifteen seconds (3:15). These two individuals may also be remembered for their Black Power salute during the awarding of medals at the 1968 Olympics.

Carlos and Seagren returned to the Gardens in 1970, and world record holder Willie Davenport also competed. More important, however, were three women who would soon be making names for themselves: Debbie van Kiekebelt, Diane Jones and Debbie Brill, who was the holder of the Canadian women's high jump record at the time.

Speed-skating at the Gardens, 1934.
ALEXANDRA STUDIO

Ten years later, the Games were still going strong at the Gardens, now sponsored by the *Toronto Star*. Entered in the 1980 meet were such stars as pole vaulter Dan Ripley of the United States, world record holder at eighteen feet, five-and-one-half inches and winner of the event during the 1979 Games. In comparison, the indoor pole vault record in 1964, the second year of the Games, was sixteen feet, eight-and-three-quarter inches. Debbie Brill repeated her 1979 high jump win, but the featured event was the mile. In this race, Filbert Bayi was bested by world record holder and winner of the 1979 Games, Eamon Coghlan of Ireland.

The Telegram-Star-Maple Leaf Games have dominated the track scene at the Gardens for almost twenty years. There have been other track and field contests, of course, such as the Tri-County Track Meet of March 3-4, 1977, which pitted the best of Canada, the Soviet Union and the United States against each other, but none has attracted as much attention as the Games. A fixture in the Toronto athletic calendar, they promise to entertain track fans at the Gardens for some time to come.

Such prominent sports as tennis and track are well known to people who frequent the Gardens, but many are unaware that badminton championships have also been staged in the building. Singles and doubles matches were held there for the first time on May 4, 1932. Jack Devlin and W. B. Jones of the Winter Club were defeated by C. W. Aikman and Jack Purcell of the Carlton Club of Toronto. Local players won all three matches. Devlin was a former British Amateur Champion, and he was roundly cheered by a fair-sized crowd that at times found the match "scintillating."

Basketball was invented in 1892 by a Canadian, Dr. James Naismith, but it never attained the stature of hockey in his home country and did not make its first appearance at the Gardens until January 16, 1946. At that time the Rotary Club staged a benefit in aid of the Hospital for Sick Children. Nearly 8,000 fans who, according to a contemporary spokesman, were "practically tearing each other's buttons off to get in" saw two interesting games. In the preliminary contest, the University of Toronto team nipped the Western Mustangs 47-46, while in the main event the professional world champions, the Fort Wayne Zollners, defeated the Rochester Royals 60-53.

The college game had a picture finish. With Varsity leading by only one point and the game at full time, a foul was called against the Toronto team. Curry of Western gave great deliberation to the foul shot, arced the ball, hit the rim and saw hope for a tie bounce away. The most valuable player of the professional game, the Zollners' Bud Jeannette, stood only 5 feet, 11 inches tall, but he scored thirteen points on skill rather than height. Flushed with success the Rotary Club organized another show on February 22 featuring Assumption College of Windsor, the Tip Tops, Dow Athletic Club and the Hayes Hellcats.

Nineteen forty-six also introduced National Basketball Association games to Gardens' fans. In a special promotion anyone taller than Toronto's six-foot eight-inch George Nostrand was admitted free. The New York Knickerbockers took on the Toronto Huskies, an NBA franchise at the time. The Huskies took a 48-44 lead at the end of the third quarter, much to the delight of the Toronto crowd, but they wilted in the last period and lost 68-66. Ed Sadowski of the Huskies was game high scorer with eighteen points.

The Huskies were only able to tie Boston for fifth place in the NBA that year, and because the club cost $125,000 a year to operate, the franchise collapsed the same year. The fans had but few opportunities to see basketball at the Gardens during the ensuing years. There were Olympic trials in 1948, and the best-known team in basketball has been to the Gardens every year since 1951, playing each time before large and enthusiastic crowds.

The Clown Princes of Basketball, the Harlem Globetrotters, began as a team in 1927. By 1978 they had played to more than 90 million people in over 13,400 career games. The first time they appeared at the Gardens nearly 14,000 delighted fans had a very good time. The Globetrotters are loved the world over for their comic performances, using basketballs as props. The 1951 game in Toronto was no exception, and Goose Tatum, who billed himself as "the greatest showman in sport," put on a dazzling show. "With hands that must be a foot long," the Goose, "did everything with the ball but swallow it," according to a news account of the time. The second game of the evening was a professional exhibition game between the Minnesota Lakers (later moved to Los Angeles) and the Philadelphia Warriors, which was won by the Lakers 63-45.

The Toronto Huskies had folded fairly recently, so these games stirred up some agitation in the city for another big league team. But the papers warned that the big turnout for the Globetrotters didn't mean that Toronto was ready for another franchise. There likely weren't enough good people like Abe Saperstein around (he brought the Globetrotters to the Gardens), nor were there enough stars in the majors like Goose Tatum.

No matter what, Gardens' fans annually delight to the antics of Curly Neal, Meadowlark Lemon, Geese Ausbie, Nate Branch and many others who have come and gone with the team over the past thirty years. Time after time the 'Trotters break their own attendance records at the Gardens. On March 30, 1979, for example, they set a new high for basketball in the building, attracting 16,850 spectators. And still they keep coming — the fans and the Globetrotters.

Professional basketball was reintroduced to Toronto on January 14, 1971, when the Los Angeles Lakers played the Cincinnati Royals. This game was the result of negotiations started nearly two years earlier. In 1969, Toronto lawyer Norman Freedman contacted the Commissioner of the NBA, Walter Kennedy, and asked if there might be a chance for a game in Toronto. Freedman argued that the time was right, because a professional match had not been held in the city for twenty-three years. He got his permission, hooked up with another lawyer, Ruby Richman, and talked Cincinnati coach Bob Cousy into playing a home game at the Gardens. The two lawyers also had in mind a possible NBA franchise for Toronto, and this was a good way to judge response.

Cousy's team had the great Nate Archibald on its roster, but the Lakers countered with Wilt Chamberlain, Elgin Baylor, Gail Goodrich and Jerry West. The crowd was elated to have the opportunity to watch such legends in action, and more games were planned. The Buffalo Braves played some of their home games in the building in 1971, 1973 and 1974, while the American Basketball Association put on a double-header early in 1972.

Inviting the Braves to play nine regular games and one exhibition at the Gardens was a further step in the experiment to determine Toronto's interest in an NBA franchise. But this time Bill Ballard was the prime mover. "It's not completely reliable as a market experiment," he said in 1973, "I mean, will people be coming to see Buffalo against Milwaukee, or will they be attracted by Kareem Abdul Jabbar? What we're finding, though, is that people who are subscribing to the first ten games are asking if they can reserve the same location next year, when we're in the NBA." Unfortunately, the interest shown just wasn't sufficient, but the possibility of a professional franchise continues to surface on occasion.

While closed circuit television has brought such spectacles as World Cup Soccer and the Indianapolis 500 to Gardens' crowds, there are other, less prominent sports staged live in the building. The 1964 Tournament of Champions Invitational Curling Bonspiel took place there, and the quality of the ice was a tribute to the Gardens' maintenance staff. Among the contestants were some of the finest players in the world: the Richardson family from Regina, Matt Baldwin of Edmonton, Doug Cameron of Charlottetown and Hec Gervais, the Briar and Scotch Cup Champion of 1961.

The International and Ontario Mentally Retarded Floor Hockey Olympics were held in the building on a number of occasions before such spectators as Pierre Trudeau and Mrs. Rose Kennedy. Volleyball,

Wilt Chamberlain (13) was one of the famous basketball players who played at the Gardens in the early 70s.

too, has appeared, with a game between the American and Soviet teams in 1965, and Japan-Canada women's volleyball after that. This sport was promoted chiefly by Anton Furlani of Toronto. Gymnastics has also been a big attraction, with the Milk Meet '76 setting a world record attendance mark for indoor gymnastics.

Much like international hockey, gymnastics and politics seem to go together. As an example, the 1980 World Cup gymnastics meet, held at the Gardens from October 24 to 26, 1980, was fraught with controversy. Since Canada had boycotted the 1980 Olympics, the Soviets were accused of not sending their best gymnasts to the meet. Possibly it's just as well, for the two world-class gymnasts that Russia did send placed first and second in their events.

Canada, while not overwhelming the competition, did provide some interesting moments. Twelve-year-old Elfi Schlegel earned Canada's first medal in the vault event when she tied for third place, in spite of a dislocated toe. The four-foot eleven-inch gymnast was the darling of the crowd, drawing a standing ovation for her 19.30 score in spite of an injury.

Finally, there has been a true sports spectacular at the Gardens. Quentin Reynolds, veteran newspaperman, reporter and foreign correspondent, hosted "The Wonderful World of Sport" between September 29 and October 4, 1964, just before the start of the year's hockey season. The world's largest tank was erected for precision swimming, water ballet and clowns. A special tower was added to accommodate a daring Acapulco cliff diver. Also on the programme were gymnastics, boomerang throwing, a West German acrobatic motorcycle team, Highland games, Thai foot-boxing, Japanese martial arts and The Mexican Aztec Flying Birdmen. This is the only time that such a variety of sports has been staged in the arena on one occasion.

There have been literally thousands of different sporting events at the Gardens during the half-century of its existence. No mention has been made, for example, of such things as the international basketball games featuring the Israeli and Mainland Chinese teams, or of such people as Richard Kihn, Slava Corn and Ed Brougham who promoted international gymnastics. In fact, relatively little has been said about gymnastics in general. There is much more to the sport of lacrosse at the Gardens, while neither soccer in the building, nor the contributions of the Toronto Blizzard to the new indoor league, has been discussed.

The focus here has been on the tremendous versatility and vibrancy of an arena that Conn Smythe originally saw as primarily an ice palace. Strong as the sporting tradition may be, the Gardens has also served as a stage for many other kinds of entertainment and a forum for a wide selection of groups.

*Frank Sinatra at the Gardens
in 1976.*
REPRINTED WITH PERMISSION FROM
THE TORONTO STAR

CHAPTER V   THE ENTERTAINERS

ENTERTAINMENT COMES IN MANY FORMS, whether big bands, singers, ice shows, comedians or even rodeos, and Maple Leaf Gardens has featured the best. Beginning with the big bands in the early 1930s, through Bob Hope, Roy Rogers, Frank Sinatra and Steve Martin, up to the current ice extravaganzas, the building has featured very impressive performances over the years. Their story reads like an outline of the changing tastes and values of North America.

Although he did not come to appear on stage, an interesting Gardens' story is told about Hollywood tough guy George Raft. Known for his portrayals of hard-bitten characters, Raft visited the Gardens once in the 1930s, only to swear he would never return. Foster Hewitt asked him to visit the gondola during a hockey game. In those days, the gondola was reached by crossing a catwalk 121 feet above the ice, then climbing down a rickety ladder that was at a 90 degree angle. Foster warned Raft to look straight ahead, not down, on the last leg of the journey, but the veteran broadcaster recalls, "I looked back and heard a thud, and there was Raft, down, hanging onto a steel plank. He'd looked down and nearly passed out. I had the worst time trying to get him back. He never, of course, actually got to the gondola."

Raft went, but the big bands started to come. Eddie Duchin's orchestra came to play at a dance that almost didn't happen. They were scheduled for September 21, 1934, but en route from the United States they were taken off the train at a Buffalo border crossing and detained by the authorities. Duchin's Central Park Casino Band was supposed to have been granted entry permits, sponsored by the Embassy Club, but the permits were sent from Ottawa to Toronto instead of Fort Erie. Finally, this snarl was straightened out, only to have their bus blow a tire. This was followed by a half-hour wait for a raised drawbridge at the Welland Canal. Even after all these delays, the intrepid group arrived at the arena only forty minutes late, to the delight of 3,000 people.

Legendary band followed legendary band. After Duchin came Paul Whiteman in 1938, followed by Duke Ellington who was involved in the first Gardens' jitterbug contest. "Votaries of St. Vitus Groan, Yelp,

Wiggle, Peck, and Truck almost threw fits to win a prize," the local media reported. The contest was sponsored by the Lions Club and called, somewhat appropriately, the "Jungle Jamboree." Some 7,000 fans were on the floor, some dancing quietly, some listening to the music and some groaned and yelped to warm up for the jitterbugging. It must have been quite a scene.

In the words of a *Globe and Mail* account, "One had only to squint slightly, listen to the throbbing rhythm of the Duke's drums, and imagination carried you away to darkest Africa." The crowd certainly appreciated the driving beat, but cheers for the dancers soon drowned out the band. The mood of the entire evening was stated succinctly by one reporter who wrote, "The lady wears trunks to match her skirt . . . because she spends fifty per cent of her time upside down. She may lie on the floor and shimmy, or even throw a fit, but that would only bring more applause." We presume that he was writing about the jitterbug contest.

During the war years, the Gardens was all but taken over by benefit concerts. As part of one such night, Paul Robeson, the "great basso," appeared on June 29, 1942. He acted as both singer and speaker at this Salute to Canada's Army. The event was attended by 10,000 spectators, and Robeson donated his time, all the proceeds going directly to the Red Cross for a mobile transfusion unit. The gift was to be presented in honour of Dr. Norman Bethune, who was at the time working in China.

Another wartime benefit took place in 1943, when the Fitch Band Wagon presented Guy Lombardo and his Royal Canadians. Long-time favourites of "sweet" dance music fans, Lombardo presented a two-hour programme in aid of the Toronto retail druggists' drive to sell $300,000 in war saving stamps. Druggists were given stickers to put on the covers of regular stamp books. A sticker meant entry to the Gardens' benefit. Purchase of a $3 stamp would ensure one of the best seats in the house, while other seats were guaranteed by stamps worth $2.50, $1.75 and $1.00. No tickets were sold at the door.

The biggest event of the war years had to be the Bob Hope Show. Hope stopped into the Gardens on one of his worldwide tours in order to support the druggists' stamp drive. On September 20, 1944 it was a toss-up who netted the most applause, Hope or the young veterans in the audience who were patients at Toronto's military hospitals. Between gags, Hope came into the audience and talked with the vets. The arena was jammed to the roof, and even standing room had been sold out long before the show. The total sale of stamps was estimated at $35,000, topping the previous record set for the benefit by Gracie Fields.

Hope was at his best. Hanging onto the microphone and chewing gum, he gave the largely civilian audience a glimpse of the kind of

Gene Autry chats with Conn Smythe and Premier George Drew during his appearance at the Gardens in 1946.
ALEXANDRA STUDIO

Roy Rogers, King of the Cowboys, visited local hospitals before his appearance at the Gardens in 1944.
ALEXANDRA STUDIO

Guy Lombardo and His Royal Canadians were popular at the Gardens during the war.
ALEXANDRA STUDIO

shows he put on for the military. He made jokes about his golf game, about Crosby and Sinatra ("He's the WAC's pin-up boy"), about the draft, and about his bets on horses ("First horse I ever saw that started from the kneeling position").

Hope's jokes were in a much lighter vein than the opening remarks by Air Marshal Billy Bishop, VC, who told the audience that, "a healthy hate for the Nazis would do neither our cause nor ourselves any harm." But the mood quickly changed when Frances Langford appeared in a slinky black dress that nearly brought the house down. Comic Jerry Colonna performed in sketches with Hope, while Alan Lund and the Navy Show rounded out the evening's entertainment.

At least one show during the 1940s turned into a benefit for the audience, because they were treated to a singing lesson and a bit of unexpected kibitzing from the spectators. The Roy Rogers Texas Rodeo took place at the Gardens from May 2 to May 6, 1944. Opening night started a bit slowly for the 12,000 fans, not counting the ushers and two members of the Toronto Maple Leafs baseball team. Rogers suggested, "Let's all sing 'Home on the Range.'" He even obliged with the first few bars, then trailed off with an embarrassed sigh. "I know what's wrong," drawled the cowboy. "Them lights is embarrassin' the older folks. Turn 'em off."

In the anonymity of the darkened arena, everyone got involved in the singing. Everyone except the ball players, that is; they sat and yelled

Bob Hope, Frances Langford and Jerry Colonna pose with two Canadian war veterans during Hope's visit to the Gardens in 1944.
ALEXANDRA STUDIO

"Fire!" at intervals. Rogers was unruffled and explained, "They're Red Kress and Harry Davis, folks. I met them on the train and told them a story that has a fire in it. Can't repeat it here, though. Take a bow, boys." After that Roy rode around the arena yelling "Howdy!" The two ball players yelled back, "Fire!"

Roy Rogers had other problems with the fans, or at least his horse did. Trigger had all of the hair pulled out of his tail by souvenir hunters over the years, and by the time he came to the Gardens, he had to wear a false tail, like a wig, to hide his baldness. He also had to have a guard to stand watch over his wig and to make sure that no one stole his hairpiece. From the war years to the time of his death, Trigger's tail was bald.

The Rodeo represented a significant achievement on the part of the Gardens. Five hundred tons of dirt had to be trucked into the building (and later out of it as well) and spread ten inches thick over the cement floor to protect Roy, Trigger and the famous $2,500 saddle. It was quite a night, what with Roy and Trigger, hecklers, steer wrestling, bull riding (in which two contestants were injured), never-miss horse-shoes and rope tricks.

Not to be outdone, the other singing cowboy of the period, Gene Autry, brought his S. Q. Ranch Rodeo to the Gardens in May, 1946. He was shown around Queen's Park by Premier George Drew, and took the time to visit the Hospital for Sick Children. At the Gardens,

Gene sang "Rudolph the Red-Nosed Reindeer," even though it was spring and raced around the floor on his horse, Champion. No one yelled "Fire!"

The interest in such gala rodeos had at least something to do with the overall drabness of the war years. In a further attempt to brighten things up, unusual shows and costumes began to become standard props in the building. In 1944, Phil Spitalny brought an orchestra to the Gardens which combined the best in visual and audial entertainment. Many of the 8,000 fans who came on opening night were surprised by his all-female band; not only were they lovely to look at, they were also good musicians. "But while the program is popular," one reviewer wrote, "there is no room for dumb beauties. This concert outfit looks like something from a revue for which the producer has not been stingy with the costume bills. It was the first time in Canada for the American girls. No place but America could produce a program with two Ave Marias and the Lord's Prayer sung by a chorus line in sequined costumes." The strange thing is, it worked.

Perhaps because the end of World War II was in sight, the year 1944 was a good one for singing and dancing at the Gardens. The immensely popular Andrews Sisters appeared on October 30, but not before Maxine, Laverne and Patty did a lot of singing around the city. They visited the Chorley Park Military Hospital and the Christie Hospital to entertain patients, and found time to attend a Victory Loan celebration at City Hall. They won the hearts of Gardens' fans by putting on "not a concert, but a thorough good time." As a *Globe and Mail* reviewer put it in the language of the day, "All the performers were bright and amiable, but by tremendous effort they achieved the moronic [?] ideal. The old hot shows were black sheep; these are as pure as lambs. But there is also a lot of bleat, and the fans go for it." After this review, what more can be said?

An appearance by Tommy Dorsey was the other high point of 1944, but strangely the crowd numbered only about 3,500. The turnout may have had something to do with the fact that he had only recently returned to the band after being on trial in the United States for rearranging the nose of movie actor Jon Hall. Dorsey had said publicly that the incident hadn't affected his popularity, but the small Gardens' crowd seemed to belie his confidence. As well, Toronto's attitude toward Dorsey might have been altered because Frank Sinatra was no longer with the band, which arrived instead with tenor Frank Stewart. He had only been singing with the orchestra for six weeks. In Dorsey's view, after Sinatra everyone else suffered by comparison. The fans apparently agreed. But Dorsey wasn't going to starve without Sinatra, because it was also known at the time that he was making at least $1.25 million per year.

A study in contrasts. Perry Como's dressing room including barber chair, for his 1957 concert.
ALEXANDRA STUDIO

Bob Hope's dressing room in 1978. Only Hope and Frank Sinatra have used the Leafs' dressing room.

Perry Como on stage at the Gardens in 1957.
ALEXANDRA STUDIO

The war ended, but benefit performances at Maple Leaf Gardens continued. They took the form of fund-raising events for institutions at home rather than a war effort overseas, but they still often had overtones of the late conflict. The Gyro Remembrance Night of January 29, 1946, for example, was staged to pay for a quiet room and library at Sunnybrook Military Hospital. The tone was set for the evening in a recorded message from the recently widowed Eleanor Roosevelt, while Alex Templeton, the noted pianist, the Toronto Symphony Orchestra under the direction of Sir Ernest MacMillan, and the Mendelssohn Choir provided a stirring musical programme.

The variety shows put on at the Gardens during the war years proved conclusively that the city wanted more of this type of entertainment. Albert College sponsored the Grand Concert held at the Gardens in 1947. Some critics seemed to think that the show had a bit too much variety, but nevertheless Alex Templeton was able to captivate the audience. Despite the critics, it was generally agreed that this was one of the most pleasant musical evenings ever put on in the building, particularly because the programme also featured Ezio Pinza of the Metropolitan Opera, who was extremely popular at the time.

For those who preferred a more ecclesiastical evening, the famous Roman Choir was booked into the Gardens in the same year. This was the first mid-August choral concert in Toronto, and the fifty-four men and boys in the choir were able to create "in the great unliturgic temple of hockey and wrestling an even greater impression than the notable Vatican Choir did at Massey Hall." This remark is interesting, both because it points out that the Gardens was still seen in terms of sports, and because it foreshadows the remarkable achievements in the performing arts which were to appear at the Gardens in the not too distant future.

Bob Hope brought comedy back into the building in 1949, telling jokes about the Canadian federal election, and was followed by another American funny man, Jack Benny, in 1950. Benny and his perennial sidekicks, Phil Harris and Rochester, amused a large crowd. In the words of a promotional piece, they were accompanied by "a gorgeous hunk of Hollywood named Vivian Blaine." The comic character traits developed over twenty years in the business were all evident in the show. At the end of the performance, there was a special announcement by Lorne Greene. Greene told the spectators that the penny-pinching Benny had visited Variety Village in Toronto and decided to completely furnish a room in this school for crippled children. So much for appearances on stage and the realities of a performer's private life. Benny had said during the show, "You can't say I don't provide you with the best," and this night he gave the best he had to offer.

By the 1950s the variety show had blossomed into an annnual event called "The Biggest Show," a fitting title for the era of the biggest and

Simpson's Teen-Town Time Dance, April 26, 1946, featuring Bobby Gimby and Ellis McLintock.
ALEXANDRA STUDIO

LEFT: *Horace Heidt and His Californians, in a publicity shot announcing their upcoming concert at the Gardens.*

RIGHT: *Liberace exchanged his glittering suit for a straw hat in a 1954 country number.*
ALEXANDRA STUDIO

the best in everything. The entry for 1951 had an all-star cast: Duke Ellington and his orchestra, Nat King Cole and Sarah Vaughan. They played before some 6,500 people, and one reviewer noted that "Sarah Vaughan has never been in such fine form as this evening, although Cole's honeyed voice depends on more intimate surroundings."

The Biggest Show for 1952 featured Stan Kenton in place of the Duke, and both of these shows pointed strongly in the direction of the rock and roll years to come. Both Cole and Vaughan went on to record songs such as "Mona Lisa" and "Broken Hearted Melody" at the beginning of the rock era. These songs appealed to a younger audience and climbed on the charts shortly before rock became popular. Gardens' audiences were witnessing a musical transition, but no one in those days could have foreseen the immense popularity of Bill Haley, or even the existence of someone like Frank Zappa.

Just as the variety show continued into the fifties, so the rodeo made several more appearances in the building. The Cisco Kid put on a show on June 6, 1952, but it was a decided flop. Cisco couldn't sing very well, and it is said that he even fell off his horse at one point, so he obviously couldn't ride very well either. But to save the day for the noble horse, Gene Autry returned in 1953. Gene was filled with complaints about his horse. "The only thing kids seem to be interested in is my horse," Gene told the audience. "Does he buck? Does he bite? I just have to take a back seat." These weren't serious complaints, though. After all, Roy Rogers ended up having Trigger stuffed, and Cisco fell off his mount, so a little attention for Champion seemed in order.

Multi-millionaire Autry led a chorus of "Rudolph," presented his sidekick, Pat Butram, had rope tricks, dog tricks and acrobatic dancing — in short, everything a rodeo needs except bucking broncos, and no one really missed them.

The days of the great cowboy personalities faded away, but the rodeo continued to come to the Gardens. These events always presented problems in a building primarily designed to serve as an ice palace. The Canadian Championship Rodeo arrived in 1963, but difficulties were created by staging it on a Friday evening. The Leafs and the Red Wings were scheduled to play hockey the next night, and six inches of clay loam had to be removed from the concrete floor before the ice could be made. The staff had only a few hours to get the dirt out, and to prepare the ice surface. Harold Ballard decided to pitch in, helping his maintenance crew with pick and shovel. "You can always hire those guys — and pretty cheap, too," he rationalized after the feat was accomplished, "but it would take a long time before I'd admit that I couldn't do something myself."

The popularity of the big bands, however, seemed definitely on the downswing with the advent of rock and roll. In an effort to balance this rising tide, the Gardens brought in Maria Callas on October 21, 1958, followed by Benny Goodman in 1959, and Fred Waring and his

Rita Pavone, singing in one of the many concerts for Italian-speaking Torontonians held at the Gardens.

Steve Martin, 1979.

Many country and western stars, including Willie Nelson, have entertained at the Gardens.
JOHN ROWLANDS

Pennsylvanians in 1960. The crowds just weren't interested in music that couldn't be heard a block away on Yonge Street, though, and even the powerful double bill of Duke Ellington and Stan Kenton couldn't fill the building in 1960. The last of the big bands played the arena in 1974, featuring Bob Crosby, Freddy Martin, George Shearing and Margaret Whiting.

The history of rock at the Gardens is covered in the next chapter, but during the years when Jimi Hendrix and Jim Morrison and the Doors reigned supreme at the Gardens, one unusual event occurred that proved that rock and roll wasn't the only popular music. In 1969, a young Frenchman named Paul Mauriat made the Gardens one stop on his North American tour. Mauriat, a pianist, had scored big with his hit single, "Love is Blue," the first instrumental to go to the top of the charts since 1963. The song was recorded on a 1968 LP, and both album and song were first played on a Winnipeg radio station. From there they were heard in Minneapolis, then soon across North America, a notable achievement at a time when rock was king.

Country music stars have appeared at the Gardens on occasion, the biggest and the best to that time likely being Johnny Cash on November 10, 1969. The concert was sold out almost immediately and broke a Gardens' attendance record with 18,106 fans and a gross of $93,000, more than for the Beatles concert. By this time, Cash had become a legend, was married to June Carter who was expecting their first child and had overcome his addiction to tranquillizers and pep pills. When asked about his attitude toward drugs, Cash replied, "I don't have any feelin' about it one way or the other. I wouldn't tell anybody not to. But if they were goin' to, I'd tell them to be careful. Because I un'erstan' it's a felony."

His concert was outstanding. Cash's personal sidekicks were all there: Carl Perkins, The Carter Family, Doug Kershaw, The Statler Brothers, The Tennessee Three, and Tommy Cash. And his songs were known to everyone, from "I Walk The Line" to "Folsom Prison Blues."

The history of the Gardens is in some ways a record of the changing face of Toronto. Over the years there have been concerts aimed at the city's Italian population, but in the late 1970s entertainers appealing to the East Indian community began appearing, including Lata Mangeshcar, a woman who had sold more records than Sinatra at that time. But Sinatra was no slouch in the record department, and when the Master came to the Gardens for the first time in 1975, he drew 36,000 people for two performances on May 10, and set a one-day record with a gross of $500,000.

The Gardens had been trying to book Sinatra for years, and when he did come the best seats in the house sold for $25 and there was no lack of buyers. During one of his shows he held up a huge card signed by the Gardens' staff wishing him luck, and in return he later gave staff members small gifts inscribed "Love and peace, Frank Sinatra." He wasn't that congenial with everyone, however. He also held up one of the local newspapers on stage, tore it into little pieces and stated that it was only fit for training dogs and lining bird cages. This incident aside, the concert was a tremendous success, as was the sold-out concert in 1976. In both years, box office records were established which are still unbroken. Regardless of the kind of publicity he received, Sinatra packed them in.

Entertainment has taken many forms at the Gardens and many different types of performers have thrilled its audiences. One type that has appealed to vast crowds is the ice show. We have to go back to 1935, long before the Ice Capades or the Ice Follies, to discover the first ice show at the Gardens. The Toronto Skating Club first appeared in March of that year and was an annual event for a number of seasons afterward.

But the forerunner of the modern ice extravaganza was Sonja Henie and Company who came to the Gardens on December 5-6, 1938. Toronto turned out 12,000 strong to welcome back its own Stewart Reburn. Only a few months before, he had gone to Hollywood seeking fame and fortune as Henie's partner. There were so many curtain calls for his performance (eight) that it was feared the rest of the show might have to be postponed. Possibly because of the graceful skating of Henie and Reburn, possibly because a home-town boy made good and returned, or possibly because of a hint of romance between the two, the crowd was on its feet all night. The couple performed a tango number, and an observer recorded, "they smiled at each other . . . and when they skidded to a stop to take their bow they held each other's hands for what seemed to be a long time." Miss Henie was "a poem of grace," and Toronto was hooked on the poetry of the ice show.

It wasn't until 1941 that the first modern ice show appeared with the arrival of the Ice Follies of Shipstads and Johnson. The crowd of 8,000 was skeptical, because although the American show was highly acclaimed in the States, Torontonians were long used to ice shows and weren't easily impressed. But the crowd was soon ecstatic — with four Canadian girls in the cast, the show wasn't five minutes old before the fans were cheering, and they didn't quit until the finale two-and-a-half hours later.

Everything was there to make the show a success: good lighting, excellent music, handsome costumes and even an occasional butterfly or wood nymph falling on its posterior. The headliners, Bess Erhardt, Roy Shipstad and Oscar Johnson were very well received, but the warmest applause was for the Swiss team of Frick and Frack. One reviewer wrote, "Taking it by and large, from north to south, from 8:30 to 11:05 p.m. the Follies is to the conventional skating carnival what *Fantasia* is to a one reel black and white cartoon." In fact, the

Follies was such a success that it has been coming back to the Gardens ever since.

The Ice Capades was formed to compete with the Follies, and it made its first appearance in the building in 1943. In American reviews, the show was described as "an entertainment must" in the *New York Times*, "ace of them all" by Walter Winchell and "gargantuan" in the *New York World Telegram*. A tough act to follow in other words, and according to one *Globe and Mail* reporter the finale came all too soon. "The skate opus glitters as a great show attested to by the salvos of applause of a jammed arena augmented by the whistling and stomping of a thousand guest airmen." There were other interesting comments, including "gobs of gorgeous girls" and "breathtaking scenic effects" which tended to get the point across. The Ice Capettes and the Ice Cadets were singled out for praise, as were the "Old Smoothies," the skating pair of Orrin Markhus (51 years old and more than 200 pounds) and Irma Thomas. Part of the proceeds were turned over to the Kiwanis Club for charitable purposes.

Both the Ice Capades and the Follies have been excellent over the years, and it has always been difficult to choose between the two. Mr. Frick, the comedian, has endured with the Follies for forty years, and Richard Dwyer, who hands out roses to the audience after each performance, has had thirty years of service with the same company. Year after year praises were heaped on both shows. In 1964, for example, Joseph Erdelyi of the *Globe and Mail* pointed out in a review of the Follies: "Beauty, youth, colour and sweet music invaded Maple Leaf Gardens . . . Canada's Donald Jackson excels." Jackson was from Oshawa, Ontario, and held the 1962 world championship and the bronze medal from the 1962 Olympics, and was BBC International Athlete of the Year. He was described as "one of the finest skaters in the history of the sport, a dazzling freestyle artist." The Ice Capades has also presented great stars: Otto and Maria Jelinek, Karen Magnussen, Jo Jo Starbuck and Dick Button to name just a few.

Barbara Ann Scott was a Canadian heroine, a world champion, an Olympic champion and a cover celebrity on *Time* magazine. If the Toronto Maple Leafs' famous "Kid Line" made Canadian boys into a nation of aspiring hockey players, then Barbara Ann Scott turned Canadian girls into a nation of hopeful figure skaters. She appeared with an ice revue in 1947 and then returned to the Gardens with the Hollywood Ice Revue in 1952. Her 1948 Olympic victory at St. Moritz had been no less spectacular than her Gardens' performances. If ever the term "Canada's sweetheart" applied to anyone, it would have to be to Barbara Ann Scott.

Although the Ice Capades and the Follies tended to dominate the skating scene in Toronto, other groups began to make inroads in the late 1940s. Among these were 1948 appearances by associations like

the Toronto Skating Club and the Rotary Club, and since then there has been a steady stream of ice shows into the building. The Hollywood Ice Revue returned in 1952 and 1954, and in the latter year Andra McLaughlin was a featured skater. She will be remembered as the skater who was later to become the wife of Leaf star and coach Red Kelly.

During the sixties, the popularity of ice shows continued to rise. The Rotary Club benefit of March 16-18, 1960, was immensely successful. It was produced by Stanley Reid and starred Otto and Maria Jelinek, Donald Jackson, Barbara Wagner and Bob Paul. With all the interest in ice shows, the Leafs were encountering a crisis. Hockey had been traditional on Saturday nights at the Gardens, but when the ice shows began week-long runs which included a Saturday night performance, the Leafs began to find themselves on the road. As well, skating stars other than hockey players were beginning to become well known. An example of this phenomenon was the World Figure Skating Tour of March 29, 1975. Among other stars were such skaters as

LEFT: *Barbara Wagner and Bob Paul, Canadian, North American, Olympic and World figure skating champions.*
DANIEL NEUMAN

RIGHT: *Barbara Ann Scott.*

ABOVE: *Canadian, World and Olympic skating champion Donald Jackson.*

LEFT: *A scene from the forty-first annual Toronto Skating Club Carnival, 1953.*

The Hungarian Rhapsody number
in the Ice Capades of 1961.

A scene from a 1950s ice show.

Toller Cranston, 1977.

Dorothy Hamill and a Torontonian who was soon to make his mark, Toller Cranston.

Cranston took his cue from this tour and proceeded to assemble his own show, the "Real Thing on Ice." It was first staged in September of 1975, with repeats in 1976 and 1977. The first day of the 1976 run resulted in another ice show box office record. No other ice star grossed more for one performance than Cranston, and before the performance he received more flowers in his dressing room than any other entertainer in the history of the building.

Ice shows will continue at the Gardens, and their spectacle makes them entertainment in every sense of the word. The many fine performers over the years have provided the quality entertainment that has always been one of the main aims of the Gardens, whether on ice or on the stage. While stars like Toller Cranston have a very large following, they have been complemented by stage performers like Paul Anka, Tony Bennett, Perry Como and Steve Martin, all of whom have appeared in the building during the 1970s.

The Steve Martin show on July 29, 1979, is worth a special look, as 17,500 people were completely charmed by his two-and-a-half hour performance. Some people paid $11.50 for seats and scalpers were selling even bad ones for $20. There were Steve Martin look-alikes in the audience, people wore fake noses, arrows through their heads and Steve Martin bunny ears. The audience was prepared, and so was Martin. Peter Goddard of the *Toronto Star* wrote a review of the performance and quoted some of Martin's funnier (or unfunnier) lines.

"What's your sign, anyway?" he asked one of the girls in the front row who was helping him with one of his not-so-magical tricks.

"Aquarius," she replied.

"I'm a feces," he replied, sending the crowd into a gale of laughter.

Goddard quoted from Martin's book, *Cruel Shoes*, and from a section called "Comedy Events You Can Do" he selected one which included "Put an atom bomb in your nose, go to a party and take out your handkerchief." But while the cruel shoes remained on Martin's feet during the act, they seemed to have been left behind at the Gardens after the performance. They were about to be thrown out by the Gardens maintenance staff when rescued by the author, and now form part of Gardens' memorabilia.

So if you see Steve Martin walking around without any shoes, don't tell him where they are. Because we have them. And we're not giving them back.

A full house to see the Beatles
in 1964.
GRAPHIC ARTISTS

CHAPTER VI   ROCK AND ROLL

IT IS WELL KNOWN that Maple Leaf Gardens has been a leader in presenting sports to Canadian audiences, but in addition there is absolutely no question that it was instrumental in bringing some of the finest rock music talent to this country. It's hard to name a significant rock band or performer, from the earliest to the latest, from the most raucous to the most sedate, that hasn't appeared in the building. Bill Haley and the Comets, the Beatles, the Rolling Stones, Neil Diamond — they've all been here, many more than once. It is a fact that the overwhelming majority of people born in Toronto after 1960 have seen at least one rock show at the Gardens, while it is also true that the calibre of performers has attracted fans from other countries.

In the 1950s, the big bands seemed to be through, although the offspring of these groups, singers like Frank Sinatra for example, would continue to be popular. Of course, what could be called "cross-over" or transitional music was presented even earlier than this, but these individuals and groups have been looked at in the previous chapter. The world had calmed down after the war years, settled into the shadowy "cold war" and the spectre of Viet Nam was still some years in the future. It was then that the post-war baby boom took over the arena. In the accepted sense of the term, "rock and roll" really arrived with the recording of "Rock Around the Clock" by Bill Haley and the Comets. They were engaged to play the Gardens on April 30, 1956.

Haley arrived during the year of the Suez Crisis. The world was in turmoil once again, and the press were eager to find an incident with which they could quench the fires of this noisy new music. But then, as now, a peaceful spirit of co-operation prevailed. During the Haley concert, and over the next twenty-five years, not one incident marred the enjoyment of the young fans and their idols in the building. Rock and roll, today called "rock," has been the biggest attraction, next to hockey, since this first concert.

When Haley ended his April 30 concert with "When the Saints Go Marching Out," an obvious reference to the appreciative Gardens crowd, he could not have known that the "saints" would come marching in again, and again. So voracious are the appetites of rock fans that during 1979 forty-five shows were booked into the building, more than the total number of home games for the Toronto Maple Leafs.

Gardens' organizers were quick to follow up on the popularity of the Haley concert, and three more shows were scheduled between it and early 1957. The first real bombshell to hit the building was "The King," Elvis Presley. Without doubt, Presley was one of the greatest stars to ever play the Gardens.

He was a most engaging man, one who did not hesitate to sign autographs or pose for photographs. It goes without saying that the adulation of his fans bordered on fanaticism. Brilliantly handled by Colonel Tom Parker, Elvis played two Gardens' shows on April 2, 1957, the top ticket price being $3.50. Between shows he amused himself like a happy youngster skate-boarding in the corridors on the dollies used to move chairs. Colonel Parker wasn't amused, though. He didn't like the Canadian taxes his star had to pay, so Elvis never returned.

These were the days of the popularity war between the gyrating Elvis and the clean-cut Pat Boone. Presley, as many people will remember, was only shown from the waist up on *The Ed Sullivan Show*, while there were no such problems with Boone who appeared in white bucks and sang inoffensive ballads. The Gardens did its part to promote the contest by booking Boone on May 25, 1957. The crowd for this concert was large, but it lacked the dynamism of Presley's. Even in those early, formative days, it was easy to see who would become the greater star, although Boone's "All-American Boy" image certainly had its appeal. His clean-cut lifestyle even extended to pre-show relaxation, warming up with Building Superintendent Don MacKenzie by tossing a baseball in the corridors.

The Gardens hosted a great many rock shows during the late 1950s, including numerous appearances by The Biggest Show of Stars and Dick Clark's Caravan. Tom Jones and Englebert Humperdinck toured with Clark at that time, but they were minor lights, not the superstars they eventually became. Still, their names and the names of other great stars like Fabian, Brenda Lee, Dion and the Belmonts, Jackie Wilson, Fats Domino and Rick Nelson strike a responsive chord with those of us who were rockers then, or are nostalgia buffs now.

Things began to change a bit in 1962 when Chubby Checker brought "The Peppermint Twist" into the building. He was the first performer to wear a Maple Leafs' sweater on stage, a prop which, incidentally, he never returned. This was the beginning of a tradition, and such stars as Elton John, the Bee Gees and ABBA would later follow suit. Sweaters or not, the 1960s carried on where the 1950s left off. The appetite for rock and roll hadn't lessened, but country music and the Hootenanny also made their appearances. The Twist and the Hootenanny have gone the way of The Fly or The Mashed Potatoes, though many of us can

FIED WANT AD SERVICE
HONE EMPIRE 8-3611
a.-5 p.m. (Mon. to Fri. only)

TORONTO DAILY STAR

MORE CLASSIFIED WANT
ADS THAN ANY OTHER
NEWSPAPER IN TORONTO

H PAID CIRCULATION **396,485** COPIES PER DAY
TUESDAY, MAY 1, 1956
SECOND SECTION

3,000 Almost Berserk in Gardens Rock 'n' Roll Orgy

ONTO'S TEEN-AGERS WERE GONE, REAL GONE last night as they stamped, whistled, squealed and hooted their
rough an evening of rock 'n roll at Maple Leaf Gardens. For two and a half hours the Gardens tottered on its founda-
s the younger set, some 13,000-strong, rocked and rolled to the fantastic sounds of the Red Prysock Rock 'n' Roll

orchestra, Bill Haley and his Comets and many other stars of this newest of musical cults. Like natives at a voodoo ritual, the
crowd writhed and reeled until their pent-up emotions burst the dam of reason and they clambered on to the stage and into
the aisles to dance. Gardens officials had their work cut out trying to keep crowd in check. "It's just unbelievable," said one

*Elvis Presley at the Gardens in 1957
with Whipper Billy Watson (left)
and Frank Tunney (right).*
ALEXANDRA STUDIO

*Conn Smythe (left) welcomes Pat
Boone to the Gardens in 1957.*
ALEXANDRA STUDIO

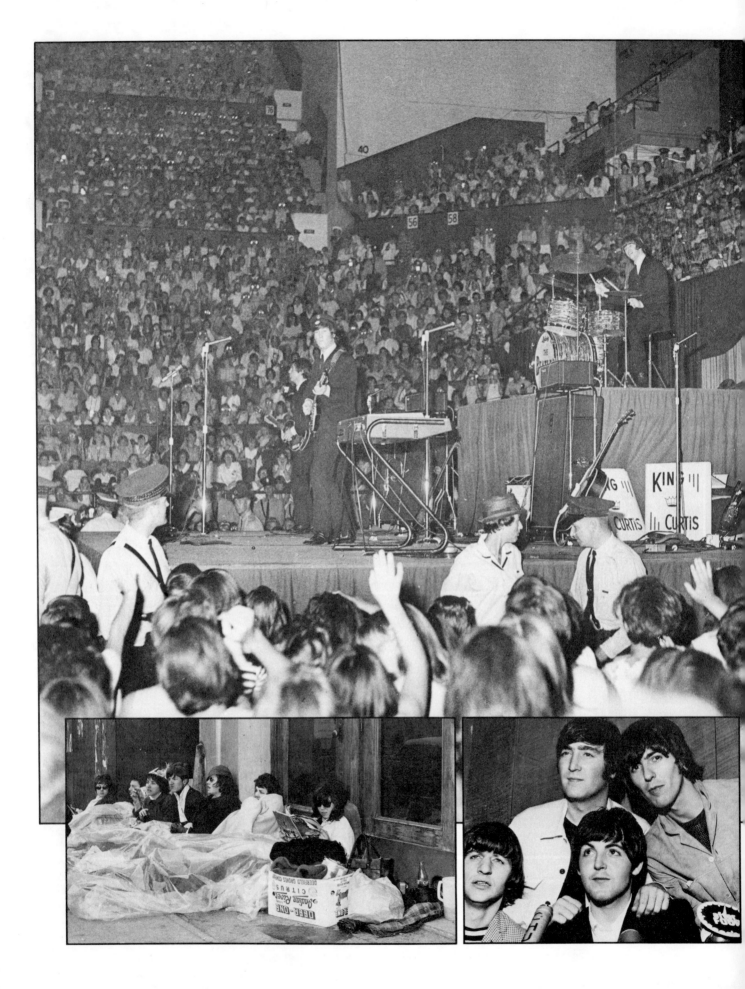

The Beatles concert, 1964.
ABOVE AND LEFT, GRAPHIC ARTISTS;
RIGHT, JOHN ROWLANDS

remember twisting and hooting with the best of them.

Bill Haley's type of rock and roll died out, replaced by the hard-driving music of Jethro Tull and Santana. The third Rock and Roll Revival concert was staged May 19, 1973 at the Gardens and featured Fabian, Dion and the Belmonts, Bill Haley and the Comets, and the Chiffons. This group was greeted by a small and rather unenthusiastic audience, a sign that the old rock was gone, and the new rock was in for an extended stay. The very fact that the concert was called a revival is indicative in itself. Some of the local newspapers didn't consider the concert of enough importance to write reviews. This was Haley's last appearance in the building, and he went into seclusion shortly thereafter until his death in February, 1981.

But the greatest rock phenomenon to sweep across the world in the sixties and into the Gardens in 1964 was The Beatles. They have dramatically affected the kind of music we have been listening to during all this time.

The fury of Hurricane Hazel was nothing compared to the storm that hit Toronto on September 7, 1964, when Beatlemania overcame the city. Even the top Gardens' officers, Harold Ballard and Stafford Smythe, donned Beatle wigs and walked up and down the long line that waited for tickets outside the building five months before the performance. Larry Zolf, of the CBC's "This Hour Has Seven Days," interviewed a man in the ticket line who was obviously in his thirties and asked him what he was going to do when he grew up. Several girls parked outside the Gardens three days before tickets went on sale, a wise strategy considering that the 18,000 tickets sold out almost immediately.

As a result, Ballard and Smythe took matters into their own hands and sold tickets for a second show, even though this hadn't been confirmed with Brian Epstein, the Beatles' manager. Fortunately, an agreement was reached and two shows were staged, one at 4 p.m. and the other at 8:30 p.m., attracting a total of 36,000 fans.

The Beatles disrupted the entire operation of the arena, even influencing the sacrosanct Stanley Cup hockey ticket sale. The great hockey immortal Charlie Conacher phoned to say, "Never mind the Leafs, get me some Beatles' tickets." CHUM radio gave roses to mothers who stood in line for their daughters. Requests for tickets came in from all over North America, and ticket sellers got into the act with their own Beatle wigs.

The performance was a smash, introduced by Masters of Ceremonies Jungle Jay Nelson of CHUM and Al Boliska of CKEY, two of the most famous disc jockeys in town. The press and publicity officer for the Beatles' Nems Enterprises said, "The Beatles have thoroughly enjoyed Toronto, and they find Maple Leaf Gardens an ideal concert venue."

It had to be ideal. In 1964, Toronto had the world's largest Beatle fan club with 50,000 members. Jane Kowicz and Wendy Woodworth, two American fans, brought Steuben crystal from Corning, New York, to give to their idols. Ray Sonin of CFRB's "Calling All Britons" claimed to be the first to play a Beatles' record in Canada. Mayor Phil Givens wandered past the group's hotel accommodations at the King Edward (they had three suites), looking for autographs. A woman from London, Ontario, tried to enter the building, saying that she was John Lennon's babysitter. The Mayor of Kingston, Ontario, showed up with a plaque to present to the foursome on behalf of the city.

Over a thousand people applied for special press courtesies. Derek Taylor, press agent for the Beatles, forwarded letters from around the world from people who wanted to attend the press conference. Paul White of Capitol Records was equally beleaguered, as were Ballard and Smythe. Americans asked the Consul General of the United States, W. Park Armstrong, to intervene on their behalf to obtain passes. One girl even wrote to President Lyndon Johnson. Big time rock and roll had definitely arrived: big names, big promotion and big gates. By comparison, the first Englishman to appear at the Gardens, Winston Churchill, attracted less than 6,000 people.

The Beatles returned to the Gardens as a group in 1965 and 1966. Later, George Harrison did a solo concert, and Paul McCartney and Wings performed, but with the tragic death of John Lennon in December, 1980, there never will be another concert like the first one in 1964.

The first Beatle concert was followed in quick succession by two more English groups, Gerry and the Pacemakers, then the Dave Clark Five. The American sound was next, with the Beach Boys, accompanied by Sonny and Cher as a warm-up act.

One of the more interesting individual personalities to appear in 1965 was Jimi Hendrix, the messiah of high-powered electric guitar fans. Hendrix flew into Malton airport for his date at the Gardens, but he was stopped by customs officials on suspicion of smuggling drugs. The Gardens arranged $10,000 bail, and I chatted with him at the Four Seasons Hotel until showtime. Although Hendrix thought about skipping both the concert and the country, he did perform that night, and was later cleared of the drug charge.

Then came the Rolling Stones, with the irrepressible Mick Jagger, giving the first of several concerts over the years on April 25, 1965. This is one of the few bands that has remained strong enough to sell out two performances ten years later. Most others of the same vintage have long faded away. Tickets for the Stones' two shows of July 15, 1972, disappeared in three hours, a total of 35,000 seats. One fan stood in line for three days, only to buy a single ticket — he could have had ten.

Rod Stewart.
JOHN ROWLANDS

Jimi Hendrix.
GODFREY JORDAN

True to form, the Stones left the fans and the media with lots to talk and write about. The show of April 25, 1965, was called "violent and vulgar" by some, "an overcrowded dog pound" by others, when a crowd of Toronto teenagers met at the Gardens for some "kicking, cursing and scratching."

The Stones made $20,000 for their night's effort, second only to the Beatles' fee up to that time. This was more amazing since the Gardens had refused to book the group a year earlier, after they had drawn only 627 fans to a concert in Boston.

They were on stage for only twenty-five minutes, during which time, according to the *Toronto Daily Star*, "they mixed obscene gestures with inaudible singing." The Stones kept beckoning the audience to rush the stage, while the police were trying to hold the audience back, and two dozen teenage girls screamed themselves into hysteria and needed medical attention.

Although they gloated over the fact that, as Stones' guitarist Brian Jones said, "We'll be leaving this town with 20,000 of your dollars in our pockets," one thing that they couldn't buy was a room at the Westbury Hotel. The hotel was frightened of the fans.

While the Rolling Stones certainly had personalities of their own, Rod Stewart had a somewhat different appeal to the audience. Stewart performed for two sold-out shows on May 6 and 7, 1979, and before the first show a woman was seen in front of the building pulling out a $50 bill to buy a ticket from a scalper. Dozens of teenage girls were milling around her, buying up $5 picture books and clutching their cameras.

"Isn't he cute?" one of the teenagers squeaked.

"He's something, honey," the older woman replied, "but cute ain't it."

A new rock music decade began on Church and Carlton with performances by Bruce Springsteen and The Who. Described by *Time* as "rock's outer limits," The Who put on two sold-out shows on May 5 and 6, 1980, and it seems that nothing can diminish their popularity.

Middle of the road music never really left the Gardens, and it seemed to be making something of a comeback in the late 1970s and early 1980s through artists such as Neil Diamond and Barry Manilow, among others. Manilow, for instance, played to a full house of mainly young, female and middle class patrons who filed into the Gardens on November 20, 1980, to hear him sing his sugar-coated songs and tell his jokes.

"I'm nostalgic," he told his audience. "When I was younger I got high on swing music and jazz. I smoked Frank Sinatra songs, snorted Count Basie arrangements, and had fantasies about all three of the Andrews Sisters and a bottle of mayonnaise."

In tribute, possibly to his fantasies but more likely to his music, fans in the Gardens held up lighted matches and lighters as he took them through the commercial jingles that he had written, while screaming, "We love you, Barry!"

The man who preferred to be alone off stage certainly didn't mind the attention on stage. "The feeling is certainly mutual," he replied softly. "This is one of the warmest audiences I've played for in a long time." With all of those burning Bics in the building, it's fortunate that the evening didn't get warmer.

Nor does the popularity of rock at the Gardens seem to be diminishing. The Rolling Stones put it best: "It's only rock and roll, but I like it."

RAMESES SHRINE TEMPLE

A scene from one of the first circus
performances in the Gardens, Bob
Morton's Circus, sponsored by the
Rameses Shrine Temple, 1934.
PRINGLE & BOOTH LIMITED

CHAPTER VII   OTHER ACTIVITIES: BENEFITS TO PAGEANTS

THIS CHAPTER WILL TRACE THE HISTORY of a potpourri of Gardens' events that don't fit into any convenient category. This variety is, in a way, a great compliment to the versatility of the old building at Church and Carlton. One day might see an ice show, rock concert or hockey game, while the next might have a benefit, military tattoo or convention. These constant and sometimes difficult transitions are a little-known facet of Maple Leaf Gardens. The next time you go to a hockey game try to imagine what the place looks like when the circus is in town.

Into this indefinable group fall such things as the first model aircraft competition held on August 4, 1932, or historical events such as the lecture given in 1935 by Admiral Richard Byrd, the first man to fly over the North Pole.

More significant than these events, perhaps, are the many benefits held in the building. They point out the central position that the Gardens has held as a venue for raising money for a variety of worthy causes from crippled children to support of the war effort.

The first Gardens' benefit was held on January 21, 1933, when the Toronto Maple Leafs played four senior hockey league teams. About 13,000 fans were admitted to the building by donating clothing to the needy victims of the Great Depression. It is often forgotten that clothing was considered a valuable commodity during these years of privation.

The Leafs defeated the Niagara Falls Cataracts 1-0, the University of Toronto Seniors 3-0, the Toronto Marlboros 3-2 and the National Sea Fleas (Allan Cup Champions) 3-0. During intermissions, the Toronto Skating Club presented comedy and figure skating demonstrations. The spectators were certainly rewarded by these exhibitions and the opportunity to help the less fortunate.

Hockey was dominant in early benefits, and some involving the Leafs, such as the Ace Bailey benefit, were mentioned in Chapter 2 of this book. However, there were other hockey benefits not discussed in that chapter. For example, on February 21, 1940, the Goodyears, Ontario Hockey Association Champions, defeated Ace Bailey's University of Toronto team 4-0 to win the city senior championship. The proceeds were turned over to the Finnish Relief Fund, which was established to aid the Finns who were then engaged in a war with the USSR.

Two years later another hockey benefit was organized, but this time in honour of an individual. Moose Ecclestone had been killed during an amateur hockey match, and a memorial fund was established to help his family. There was lots of action for the nearly 14,000 fans, the primary attraction being a speed-skating contest between professional hockey players. Syl Apps of the Leafs had to go through a skate-off with Lynn Patrick of the New York Rangers before winning the competition. The main event was a twenty-minute exhibition game where a collection of All Stars managed to tie the Leafs 3-3. It was a successful benefit, all in all, with a cheque for $9,800 presented to the fund by G. R. Cottrelle, President of the Gardens.

Among the many benefits held in the building during World War II, there were very few that were not of a political nature. These functions have been reserved for discussion under politics in Chapter 10. However, it might be worth recounting here a benefit that took place on February 18, 1944, which gives some indication of the tenor of the times. Quentin Reynolds spoke on behalf of the Food Industry War Savings Stamp Drive, and he told the audience that he hoped "that when this war is won our people will go to the peace table with hatred in their hearts." He was "annoyed and frightened" to find the people blaming only the German leaders. "I am glad to be called an apostle of hatred," he announced. "Ask your fighting men what they think of the German people."

Reynolds had spoken to the Press Club earlier in the day and had warned them that the war would not end in 1944 as many people thought. Still, it was only his faith in General Eisenhower that led him to believe that the war would not continue for many more years. He revealed that he had also learned from an unnamed source that the Germans had built an impervious 1,800-mile wall from Norway to Spain. He finished this rather irregular address by adding that, "The Russians will be very easy to do business with. They will be as sincere, honest and friendly in peace as they have been in war."

Of a less contentious nature was the Manitoba Flood Relief benefit of May 26, 1950. The presence of nearly 15,000 people was probably a direct result of public awareness of just how devastating the flood really was. Altogether the crowd donated $25,336.50 to aid the victims and were treated to performances by George Formby, Fred Waring and his Pennsylvanians, the Leslie Bell Singers and actor Jack Carson. The programme was broadcast across the country by radio and included a number of people who had been flooded out by the Red River. One man graphically described fields of dead and dying livestock, houses under

A reception in honour of Col. Harry McGee's fiftieth year with the T. Eaton Co., August 1934.
PRINGLE & BOOTH LIMITED

Re-creating Allied manoeuvres in the Gardens at one of the many rallies held during the war to promote the sale of Victory Bonds.
ALEXANDRA STUDIO

Members of the Shrine Temple, which has sponsored many circus performances at the Gardens, pose with a star of the 1934 show.
PRINGLE & BOOTH LIMITED

water or washed away and "a dark brown river gone crazy." The audience couldn't ignore the way the performers clenched and unclenched their fists as they appealed for funds, nor could they pass by the moving statement, "This broadcast has shrunken the continent to the size of a human heart."

More recently, Harold Ballard has donated the use of the Gardens for benefits on many occasions, some more successful than others. On September 19, 1972, for example, the United Appeal staged a gala evening to launch their six-week crusade for funds. The 48th Highlanders played "Amazing Grace," Sylvia Tyson sang "Give to the World," and Peter Appleyard contributed a performance. Many dignitaries were on hand, but only 1,250 people showed up, perhaps because advance publicity was lacking.

The Gardens has also been a centre for service club conventions, the first in the thirties organized by the Independent Order of Oddfellows and a number of lodges of the Association of Rebekah Assemblies. They blocked traffic for over an hour during their march from Queen's Park to the arena, where more than 7,000 people attended the 110th annual convention and witnessed a series of "vivacious" displays.

The first truly "big" convention to come to Maple Leaf Gardens was the Rotary International held in 1942. This was the club's thirty-third annual event, and it attracted more than 8,000 people from twenty-five countries. The Earl of Athlone, Governor General of Canada, gave the keynote address, and the programme included performances by Gracie Fields, Mona Bates and the Toronto Symphony Orchestra.

It is surprising to realize today that the Rotary was functioning in occupied countries in the midst of the war. Delegates were heard who represented Free France and Nanking, while a letter was read from Occupied France, arriving via the Underground, congratulating the club on the opening of the convention. The war was very much on the minds of the conventioneers, and each one was asked to contribute a dollar toward the purchase of fighter planes.

It was generally agreed that this particular convention was "the most friendly of all," due in large part to the reaction of the city. "Every streetcar driver and motorman, every taxi driver, every policeman . . . has done their darndest to take care of the visitors" is the way one delegate put it. The Rotarians also did their part for friendliness, staging an ice carnival in honour of President Carbajal of Peru; it was the first such show he had ever seen.

The Kiwanis Club convention of July, 1961, certainly was the largest in the city's history. Said an American from Ohio, "I've never seen any place in the States like it," referring to the arena itself, and the orchestras, choirs, bands and personalities that gathered to welcome the delegates to Toronto. One speaker, Lester Pearson, later the Prime Minister of Canada, took a serious stance and told the Kiwanians, "The

The International Grand Prix of November 1976.
ICE PHOTO STUDIO

knowledge of the awfulness of nuclear war exerts a restraining influence on nations." In a lighter moment Mayor Nathan Phillips of Toronto reminded the American representatives that, "Canadians were really responsible for the White House in Washington; they burnt it down."

In July of 1964, Lord Thomson of Fleet addressed the Lions Club gathering at the Gardens. Governor George Wallace of Alabama also spoke, flanked by a dozen security guards. Mimi Hines was one of the entertainers, and in a reference to the sweltering heat outside she told the maintenance staff to "throw another log on the air conditioner."

Of course, conventions haven't always been annual happenings in the building. We have already seen that sports events, like the Globetrotters and track meets, have established a yearly schedule, but in a musical sense the Toronto Police Concert has also been held annually, beginning back on February 16, 1945. The police have brought some truly great entertainment into the building, usually backed by the Toronto Symphony and a guest conductor such as Arthur Fiedler, Seiji Ozawa or Ron Goodwin. Tony Bennett was once a featured performer, and he, along with many other stars, has helped the Toronto police raise a great deal of money for the Ontario Society for Crippled Children.

Not to forget the military, there have been some dazzling and inspiring regimental bands and tattoos at the Gardens, presented by Sol Hurok of opera and ballet fame and Columbia Festivals. The Black Watch, the Argyll and Sutherland Highlanders, the Coldstream Guards, the British Tournament and Tattoo and many others have come to play before large crowds. These are regimental names that will always have a place in British military history. However, one of the problems created by military protocol has been to find a high-ranking military personage to take the salute. To this end, military figures like General Sir Neil Ritchie, General Guy Simmonds and Brigadier Denis Whitaker have graciously agreed to take part.

Under the general heading of "other activities," there have even been dog races and shows in the building over the years. These may not be as inspiring as a military band, but they are interesting to some segments of the population. The first time dogs were featured in the building was in May of 1938. Greyhounds were supposed to race on the first of two nights, but the mechanical rabbit wouldn't work. Attendance was low even on the second night in spite of an "international costume parade" in which owners wore costumes native to their dogs' homelands. The only Canadian dog, a husky, won first prize for its owner, dressed as a Canadian. Feats by Hans the Wonder Dog included such accomplishments as "rescuing a child from a burning building."

It wasn't until 1971, nearly thirty-three years later, that the second and last dog show came to the arena. Carl Noylander was the driving force behind "A Canine Extravaganza" that attracted 700 owners from Canada and the United States and at least 1,000 purebred dogs. A total of 104 breeds were represented. Seventeen judges were present to evaluate the key events, including two licensed obedience trials, demonstrations and a children's showmanship event.

Dogs have entertained at the Gardens, as have horses. The famous cowboy horses, Trigger and Champion, were mentioned in Chapter 5, but horses have also contributed to the enjoyment of spectators at circuses, and even on their own.

The most important such event was the show put on by the Spanish Riding School of Vienna on May 12, 1964. In the words of one reviewer, "It made us appreciate a new dimension of the horse." Trained by the famous 400-year old school, these stallions put on the greatest procession of horse flesh ever seen in the city. With the legendary resourcefulness of the Gardens' staff, the building was made to resemble the famed Vienna theatre, and special stalls were constructed to house the twenty-nine precious white beasts. Head trainer Colonel Alois Podhajsky was joined on opening night by the Austrian

Ambassador, Hans Leitner, and the Austrian Trade Delegate, Frederick Stockinger. The Gardens gave Colonel Podhajsky a special gift, while Columbia Festivals of New York, the group that promoted the show, presented him with a car.

The success of this extravaganza inspired an American group to bring a competitive show to the arena in 1971 which was called the Royal Lipizzan Stallion Show. These were not the same horses or the same riding school as had been seen in 1964. Even though lawsuits were contemplated because of the similarity of presentation, the show went on without any difficulty. There have been other riding events, such as

Rallies were held at the Gardens during the war in support of the Soviet Union's war effort. One such rally was the "Tribute to the Ukraine."
ALEXANDRA STUDIO

Boy Scouts, Wolf Cubs and Girl Guides often staged pageants at the Gardens. Here, Wolf Cubs perform for the audience during the 1950s.
ALEXANDRA STUDIO

the Grand Prix in 1976, although nothing has ever compared with the Spanish Riding School of Vienna.

But the horses that appeared along with circuses at the Gardens have done their best to put on a good show nonetheless, even going so far as to walk down to the floor from the third tier of seats. This feat was accomplished when the Moscow Circus came to town in 1977, and it was intended to simulate a mountain ride. This is characteristic of the circus; the unexpected becomes the commonplace. The Gardens has certainly had its share of the unexpected when it comes to circuses.

Bob Morton's show was the first to be booked into the building, appearing late in 1935 and attracting crowds of over 12,000 each night of the run. The most popular performers were Wilno the Human Cannonball, who allowed himself to be shot from one end of the building to the other, and Anna, a young lady only twenty-one inches tall who circled the arena on ringmaster Morton's arm, waving to the crowd.

Human interest stories connected with the circus are legion, and one of particular poignancy concerns Maple Leaf Gardens. Dr. Herman Ostenmaier, a native of Germany and a Ph.D. in philosophy, had trained the horses in the Shrine Circus that came to the Gardens in 1937. He had led a checkered career, once owning a large chemical business in Germany, but losing it due to unknown circumstances. Shortly thereafter he became ill, but upon recovery he decided to take a course in veterinary medicine and begin a new career. This led him to enter show business and travel the world with the circus; however while he was on the road his wife died, and he couldn't raise the money to return to Germany. Still out of money and with his wife's funeral long past, he was trying to fulfill a promise to a friend that he would bring his horses back to Germany after the Toronto booking so that they could perform at home. At this point we lose track of him. He didn't know where the funds would come from, or how he would get there. With the war coming and no further record of this tragic man, one can only guess at his fate.

The Gardens has hosted all of the world's great circuses at one time or another, including Ringling Brothers, Barnum & Bailey and Ian Garden's Canadian Circus, to name a few. As well, Don Ameche's International Playtime Circus was extremely popular, in part probably because of the ringmaster's personal magnetism. Behind the scenes he was a charming man who was driven to Mass each day and then to E. P. Taylor's horse farm near Oshawa, likely to discuss horses, their common interest.

Another entry into the world of the unexpected occurred when the Moscow Circus on Ice came to the Gardens in October of 1970. One of the acts had Siberian and Himalayan bears playing hockey. It was suggested that the Leafs play an exhibition game against the bears, but

Coach King Clancy didn't think that was a good idea. "Them bears, they don't even have to lay on the lumber. One paw, wham, it's good-bye Charlie." Carl Brewer was convinced to don a Leaf sweater and pose with one of the animals, but he never did get too close.

The circus, of course, has been the delight of many people, both adults and children, over many years at Maple Leaf Gardens, but we must not forget to mention the contributions that the children themselves have made to the rich history of the building. Especially during the 1930s, before "name" entertainment came to dominate the stage, children were very much a part of Gardens' activities. Thousands enjoyed a colourful Independent Order of Foresters pageant in April of 1934. It was called "Lilies of the Empire" and celebrated the Foresters' Silver Jubilee. The Gardens was packed to the roof to watch marching groups of children, bands and members of the Order in a spectacle that lasted more than three hours.

Children seemed to be doing the most to help Toronto celebrate its centennial year of 1934. On April 28 a Girl Guide rally was held which was described at the time as a "pageant of light and colour." Over 14,000 people watched as 3,500 put on a dazzling show, and Lieutenant-Governor Herbert A. Bruce took the salute as the girls marched past to the strains of "Rule Britannia."

Also to celebrate the centennial, the Separate Schools staged a pageant the following month. The theme was "The Old Home Town and How It Grew," and for more than three hours the arena was a background for groups of youngsters "who were temporarily transformed into Aboriginal redskins, French courtiers, Italian and Hungarian folk dancers, and were disguised as tulips, daisies, bunnies and mice." A mass gymnastics display featured nearly 800 participants.

Not to be outdone, the Boy Scouts also held a centennial celebration at the Gardens in May of 1934. Over 3,000 Boy Scouts, Sea Scouts and Wolf Cubs participated, and they even allowed the Girl Guides to join in. Lord Bessborough, Canada's Governor General and Chief Scout, spoke to the assembly in these words, "I'm going to tell you a secret. Of all the Canadians I have met in my three-and-a-half years in Canada, I like you the best." There is no record of how other Canadians he had met reacted to this statement, but in any case both he and the large crowd of spectators certainly seemed to enjoy themselves.

Although this chapter has been a potpourri of happenings in the building over the years, it does serve to show that the Gardens has been much more than an ice palace during its history. When the Gardens' day is done, as it must be some day, and a new arena is built in Toronto, the people who have been associated with the building can rest assured that they have given the city the best that Canada and the rest of the world have to offer. And this is no small achievement.

An opera performance at the Gardens.
ALEXANDRA STUDIO

CHAPTER VIII THE PERFORMING ARTS

MAPLE LEAF GARDENS has been much more than a sports palace and general entertainment centre. Before opera, theatre or ballet appeared at the O'Keefe Centre or the Royal Alexandra Theatre, the performing arts were very much alive at Church and Carlton streets. In fact, the success of such cultural activities in the building may have been one reason for the construction of the O'Keefe. During the 1950s, opera at the Gardens provided some of the supreme moments in the history of the arena and the history of cultural life in Toronto. Not only did it transform the building, it also altered Toronto society.

The Gardens was the first arena in the world to produce opera, an ambitious undertaking that set a North American pattern which was to provide an alternative to the traditional subsidized opera houses of Europe. The Canadian grand opera season opened on October 14, 1936, with *Aida* and then *Faust*. These performances were the first to be staged in the building and were the forerunners of the great Metropolitan Opera tours that came to the Gardens during the late 1950s.

Although *Aida* was one of the best performances to come to the city up to that time, it was not without its problems. The very size of the arena led to poor acoustics, the performance started late and pre-show promotion had not been adequate. Toronto opera buffs had only been informed of the show a few days beforehand, with the result that a small crowd of only 2,000 showed up for opening night. Nevertheless, Anna Leshaya of Chicago, as Aida, and Sydney Rayiner, as Rhadames, staged a brilliant performance, and the audience was enthralled. Despite the Depression, the people still managed to afford ticket prices of $1.65, $1.15, 85 cents, 60 cents and 30 cents. There is little doubt that such operas raised the spirits of the city during the austere 1930s.

Opera did not return to the building for nearly twenty years when, on May 26, 1952, *Aida* was performed by the great Metropolitan Opera of New York. Twelve thousand patrons flocked to opening night, the first appearance of the Met in Canada since 1902. The schedule also included *La Bohème*, *Carmen* and *Rigoletto*, and during the week a record opera audience of 43,344 attended. This was the largest audience in the history of the Met up to that time.

This performance of *Aida* featured Blanche Thebom and Robert Merrill. Eleanor Steber, Jan Peerce and Patrice Munsel were heard in *La Bohème*, Rise Stevens and Merrill in *Carmen*, and Richard Tucker and Leonard Warren in *Rigoletto*. With stars of this stature, it is little wonder that there was record attendance.

The Gardens' staff had learned something from the acoustical problems encountered earlier, but at first there were a few difficulties with the special microphone system that had been installed. These were quickly ironed out. In the words of a contemporary observer, the Gardens had been converted "as far as possible" into a giant opera house; the stage occupied nearly the entire north end of the arena. It was estimated that there were 11,500 seats available for each show, but so popular was the schedule that some people ended up in the standing room area where the performance could be heard but not seen.

Despite the microphone system, the vastness of the Gardens still created echoes or could make hearing difficult, and the facial expressions and slight gestures of the performers were lost to the onlookers, except to those sitting close to the stage. For other patrons, it was like watching opera from a block away. One criticism of Robert Merrill on opening night was that his voice "wobbled" a little, no doubt due to the acoustics, but this and other technical difficulties were eventually remedied to a large extent.

On the second night of the run, 12,000 fans showed up to watch *La Bohème*, and the audience was more demonstrative at curtain call than it had been on opening night. The third evening was a triumph as 13,000 spectators, a world single-night record for opera, acclaimed Rise Stevens in *Carmen*. Miss Stevens was described as the "tempestuous, alluring gypsy girl to the fingertips . . . a sight to behold." On this night the Rotarians, who sponsored the show, sold seats not only in the standing room area, but also in the passageway above the ground floor.

By the time the Met's first run was over, it was obvious that opera would become a regular feature at the Gardens. However, to most people the reception given it in Toronto was nothing short of incredible. In their books *Opera Caravan* and *The Metropolitan Opera*, authors Quaintance Eaton and Francis Robinson indicated their amazement that opera lovers were able to overcome what might have been called acoustical sacrilege. One comment, possibly long-remembered after other praises had been forgotten, came from Rudolf Bing, General Manager of the Metropolitan Opera Company. When asked what he thought of opera at Maple Leaf Gardens, he replied, "Better than ice hockey at the Metropolitan." In any case, the calibre of the performances staged in the building meant that they were just too good to be missed.

The Metropolitan Opera.
ALEXANDRA STUDIO

*Mr. and Mrs. Robert Amell
(left) and Mr. and Mrs. Conn
Smythe arrive at the Gardens for
a Metropolitan Opera Company
performance of* Aida, *May 28, 1956.*
ALEXANDRA STUDIO

Stanley Reid of the Rotary Club and cultural leaders such as Mr. and Mrs. Floyd S. Chalmers were obviously pleased with the first visit of the Met. Promoter Nicholas Koudriavtzeff, who has brought many attractions to the Gardens, was so impressed that he took the company on to Montreal. In the final analysis, though, the success of this opera schedule was reflected in the fact that the Met returned yearly until 1960.

There were many high points and unusual sights in the Met's nine years at the Gardens. Hockey players like Billy Harris and Frank Mahovlich were seen in tuxedos. There was even talk that Toronto might be able to support its own opera company, especially after the 1956 schedule featuring Roberta Peters and Leonard Warren attracted 45,000 people over one week. But the end of opera at the Gardens wasn't so far in the future as everyone had thought.

Various criticisms were levelled at the 1956 schedule, even though *La Bohème* was described as a major triumph. There were weaknesses in some of the other performances, possibly because the troupe had been on an extended tour, and possibly because the company may have looked on Toronto as something of a vacation stop during their gruelling schedule. When Sol Hurok, the famed New York impresario, brought his darling, Maria Callas, to the Gardens on October 21, 1958, the cracks in the wall of operatic loyalty seemed to be widening. As one patron expressed it, "How many white shirts is a man expected to have?"

The Met last appeared at the Gardens in 1960, and by then expenses were becoming so high that the company could not realistically continue touring. Even substantial grants from wealthy Torontonians and the superb efforts of the Rotary Club could not resurrect the annual visit, and nearly a decade of fine opera at the Gardens came to an end. Today, it is unfortunate but true that opera at the Gardens is financially out of the question. But it *was* magnificent.

The 1950s were a watershed for cultural activities at the Gardens. During the same period that opera was at its height, the building also staged a performance by the illustrious Old Vic Company from Britain. From December 14 to 16, 1954, audiences thrilled to Shakespeare's *A Midsummer Night's Dream*, directed by Michael Benthall. A special nocturne was composed by Frederick Ashton, who would later return to the Gardens with the Royal Ballet, but as Sir Frederick. Robert Helpmann, Moira Shearer and Stanley Holloway led a huge Old Vic Company of 150 actors to the Gardens' stage. Patrons watched the play for a top ticket price of $6.00, about the same as was being charged for opera at the time.

Opening night was black tie only, and the cream of Toronto society mixed with other less prominent but equally interested theatregoers. This was the first and only theatre staged at the Gardens, and one of the stage attendants was heard to say, "I don't think they'll ever be able to put it on skates."

Skates or not, Moira Shearer was "majestic" in the title role, according to *Globe* reviewer Ralph Hicklin, a view echoed by other critics during the Old Vic's North American tour. The play was only loosely based on Shakespeare, yet the tour had grossed over $1.5 million by the time it reached the Gardens. In the end, though, these performances made it clear that the Gardens was not a suitable building for intimate theatre.

Though theatre wasn't as successful as opera, it is worthwhile to point out that the ambitious plans of the Gardens spawned some of the more famous theatres and auditoria across Canada. But this tradition of cultural excellence did not stop with these two performing arts; it continued with the ballet.

Like opera, ballet came early to the arena, then disappeared until the 1950s. Unlike the former art, however, these years marked the rise of ballet rather than its demise. Until 1974, almost forty years after the Radio City Ballet appeared in October of 1935, ballet was often performed at the Gardens. The Radio City programme featured a 100-piece orchestra under the direction of Reginald Stewart and different performances on each of two nights. The arena had been "skillfully remodelled for the occasion," and a highlight for Toronto audiences was the fact that twenty home-town girls danced in the chorus line, something the local press was quick to report.

To contemporary observers, the "Ballet Classique" was the most artistic dance of opening night; it was "executed with precision and great charm." Stewart's most effective selections seemed to have been Tchaikovsky's *1812* Overture and a dance from *Faust*, but there were many different opinions of the music, depending on where the listener happened to be sitting. One reviewer wrote that nothing he heard

Part of an advertising brochure for A Midsummer Night's Dream, *1954.*

altered his opinion that classical music was not suited to arenas of such size. Still, it did produce an "interesting" effect and of all the numbers, the "noisier" music was deemed the most acceptable.

This must have been a point well taken, for ballet didn't return to the Gardens for nearly twenty years. Then, in October of 1953, Sadler's Wells, one of the world's great companies, opened for a three-night run of Tchaikovsky's *The Sleeping Beauty* and *Swan Lake*. The best seats in the house afforded a close-up view of such stars as Margot Fonteyn and Rowena Jackson, and the entire run was met with unalloyed critical acclaim. At the time, Sadler's Wells was on its third tour, just having finished thirteen weeks at the Opera House in London, England. Margot Fonteyn had recently appeared as guest artist with troupes in Denmark, Paris and Spain, and the chance of seeing one of the world's prima ballerinas was enough incentive for any Toronto ballet patron to attend the performance.

Fonteyn had had a truly remarkable career, joining Sadler's Wells when just fourteen and reaching the rank of soloist within one year. Her virtuosity seemed to know no bounds on the Toronto stage, and although she called the Gardens a "cavern," no one could possibly hold it against her. Her legendary abilities helped to make opening night "an exciting and memorable evening," according to the Toronto press.

After this triumph, Sadler's Wells continued to be popular with ballet patrons, returning two years later for a second run during the bitterly cold December of 1955. Closing night was probably the best and was enjoyed by over 6,000 people. The success at the Gardens encouraged one of the Sadler's Wells managers to declare, "This has been a wonderful run in Toronto. The company enjoyed every moment of it."

Despite the ever present acoustical problems, these appearances of Sadler's Wells whet the appetites of Toronto patrons. The company came back in 1958 and 1965 with the intervening years filled with visits from some of the world's greatest ballets. Dance was popular at the Gardens during these years partly because there was no other building capable of mounting such large and complex performances. Another, perhaps more important reason was that the Gardens had a policy of booking only the best in the world, and therefore Church and Carlton was the place to be for the performing arts. In any case, ballet and the Gardens seemed to attract each other, and over nearly twenty years, from 1953 to 1974, no fewer than thirty-four companies performed in the building with runs of from one night to one week.

By the time Sadler's Wells returned in 1958, it had been named the Royal Ballet. This occurred in March of 1957 when the Royal Charter was presented to the company, under the patronage of Her Majesty the Queen and with Princess Margaret as President. At the same time Sol

Alla Osipenko of the Leningrad (Maryinsky) Kirov Ballet performs in Swan Lake, *1961.*

ABOVE: *A 1950s performance by Sadler's Wells Ballet at the Gardens.*

LEFT: *Margot Fonteyn of the Sadler's Wells Ballet, 1953.*

TOP: *The Japanese Cherry Blossom Dancers perform in the Ontario Folk Arts Festival, 1967.*
ALEXANDRA STUDIO

Hurok was made an Honorary Commander in the Order of the British Empire. A flamboyant and generous man, Hurok was once asked what he estimated the attendance to be at one performance of the Royal at the Gardens. His answer was: "Mr. Hurok has only sold-out houses."

The performance of the Royal on June 8-10, 1965, was a combination of brilliant dancing and controversy. The Royal presented a fifty-minute version of Shakespeare's *A Midsummer Night's Dream*, and it was delightful entertainment. Unfortunately, only about 4,500 patrons saw the performance, which was regrettable, and it was an indication that with the construction of theatres, ballet in the building was becoming a thing of the past.

But the ballet did not go off without a hitch. Rudolf Nureyev was quoted as criticizing dancer Svetlana Beriosova in her opening night performance of *Swan Lake* for "dancing like she had her galoshes on." However, Nureyev later claimed that he didn't say "she," but rather "they," his barb being directed at a dance quartet in the first act.

Grant Strate, resident choreographer of the National Ballet of Canada, remarked to Nureyev that the Polonaise sequence in the first act was poorly done, and that he couldn't believe that Sir Frederick Ashton had choreographed it. "He didn't," said Nureyev. "I did. But you're right. It is awful."

Ballet at the Gardens began to develop a truly international flavour during the fifties. The London Festival Ballet appeared in 1954, the Royal Danish Ballet in 1956, then the Moiseyev Dance Company from the USSR in 1958. The Moiseyev made its home in Moscow's Tchaikovsky Opera Hall where it ran a school in conjunction with the Bolshoi. It came to Toronto riding high on a tide of critical acclaim. The *New York Times* observed, "To play safe, let us risk understatement and call it merely stupendous." Igor Moiseyev was unquestionably a man of genius, and his dancers left the Toronto audiences open-mouthed. As good as the Moiseyev company was, its performance paved the way for even more glorious moments from the Bolshoi.

When the Bolshoi first came to the Gardens in 1959, it was a box-office sensation. Ticket requests came in from all over Canada and the United States. This was only the second appearance of the troupe in the West, and people were eager to see this world-famous company. At the time, the immortal Galina Ulanova danced with the Bolshoi, and at forty-nine she was still considered one of the best ballerinas in the world. However great she was, two new dancers, Maya Plisetskaya and Nina Timofeyeva, stole some of her thunder and had the audience on its feet throughout the performance. At one point Ulanova fell, but it was the most graceful fall ever seen in the building. The accident happened, so the Russians claimed, because the Gardens' stage was too short.

Mazowsze, the Polish Song and Dance Company, was a Gardens' favourite in the 1960s and 1970s.

Barely two months after the Bolshoi left, the Soviets brought the Russian Festival of Music and Dance to the Gardens. It was such a great ensemble that it provoked arguments over whether the Festival was in fact better than the Bolshoi. It was a contest between sheer exuberance and sheer beauty. The Festival was a whirling spectacle of the best dancers from Russia, Georgia, Armenia, Kazakhstan, Uzbekistan and the Ukraine, and the ability to discuss the relative merits of this company and the cream of Russian ballet was a rare gift for Toronto audiences.

Nineteen fifty-nine was truly a tremendous cultural year for Toronto, one that ended in November with the Gardens' appearance of the Polish State Folk Ballet, simply called Slask on subsequent visits. This company was the idea of one man, Stanislaw Hadyna, and it became the third successive Slavic smash hit in Toronto during 1959.

There seemed to be no end to what the Russians, Ukrainians and Poles could do, and Toronto audiences loved every minute of it. The Georgian State Ballet visited in 1960, the Moiseyev again in 1961, and the Red Army Singers and Dancers during the same year. Despite all this glamour, the Russians warned, "If you think the Bolshoi is good, wait until you see the Kirov." Toronto had the opportunity at last in October of 1961, and the company was simply superb. It was graced by such stars as Natalia Makarova, Yuri Soloviev and Vladilev Semenov. Of course, by this time the great Kirov dancer Nureyev had already defected, and Toronto audiences had to wait for a visit of the Royal Ballet in 1965 to see him perform.

The Slavic dance troupes continued to come to the Gardens. In 1961, the Polish State Song and Dance Company arrived in December. This group was the rival of the famous Slask, and through its efforts the West came to know the unusual rhythms of Poland's many folk dances, the brilliance of its national costumes and the wit of some of its lesser known authors. The Polish State Song and Dance Company was also known as Mazowsze, and when it appeared in London, England, Arnold Haskell, one of Britain's foremost dance critics and then Director of the Royal Ballet School, was led to comment: "I have suffered such agonies of boredom and irritation from folk dancers, both real and bogus, that there must be many who feel as I do. It would be a pity if they were to miss this admirable performance." Toronto's critics contributed similar views, and the company thrilled Gardens' audiences four more times between 1961 and 1976. The Gardens was booking only the best in the world, and the usual barriers between ballet and folk dance were being lowered.

The Soviet Union was beginning to send more and more cultural emissaries abroad, and their presence at the Gardens even attracted pickets to Carlton Street from time to time, for example during the visit of the Ukrainian Dance Company in 1962, but fortunately serious incidents were avoided.

Such groups as the Ukrainian Dance Company or its Hungarian equivalent that appeared in 1966 represented individual areas or countries, but not until the Ontario Folk Arts Festival of 1967 did the best of many ethnic groups assemble for a truly international performance. Russians, Poles, Ukrainians, Filipinos, Greeks, Irish and Japanese contributed national dances commemorating everything from the harvest to the coming of spring. It was a great showing of both the diversity of heritage and the unity of the world's peoples.

To mark Canada's centennial, the Bolshoi returned to the Gardens in August. The company contained an even greater assembly of talent than during the previous visit and because of the importance of the year for Canada, even the Russian Minister of Culture, Madam Furtseva, a relative of the former Soviet premier Nikita Khrushchev, came over for a press conference.

But all was not well with ballet in Toronto. The 3,000 to 3,500 patrons who turned out for the Bolshoi's last appearance at the Gardens witnessed what was described by various reviewers as a torpid dance viewed by an apathetic audience. "The ballet is simply not worth the trouble," one critic wrote, complaining about the opening night rendition of *Don Quixote*. While the stage was spacious, the conditions were not ideal, and it is not surprising that the 150 musicians and

A scene from Timmy's Easter
Parade of Stars for the Easter
Seal Campaign, March 30, 1958.
GRAPHIC ARTISTS

The Moiseyev dancers, one of the
many colourful Russian dance
ensembles to appear at the Gardens.

performers would never again see the inside of the building from the stage.

For the next few years other Soviet troupes continued to be remarkably successful in the building, so much so that the Gardens became its own impresario. Under a company called Blue and White Attractions, the Gardens booked the Georgian State Song and Dance Company in 1969 after Harold Ballard and Bob Giroux had travelled to the Soviet Union to negotiate with the group. A reception for the Georgian dancers was held in Ottawa headed by Mitchell Sharp, Canadian Secretary of State, and the Soviet ambassador. During the same year, the Osipov Balalaika Orchestra staged a performance which was well received by Toronto critics and fans. One reviewer wrote, "All was performed with the professional smoothness we have come to expect of cultural exports from the Soviet Union," a sentence that sums up rather well the performances of Russian dance groups at the Gardens over the preceding decade.

Despite all this, the years of the great ballet and dance companies at the Gardens were coming to an end. The Mazowsze group returned for its fifth and final visit in February of 1976, and this was the last of the companies to be seen in the building. Appropriately, the Polish Ambassador, Josef Czesak, threw a large reception at Toronto's Sir Nicholas Restaurant, and the Gardens contributed part of the proceeds of the show to the Reymount Foundation, the Adam Mieckiewicz Fund, Lublin University and for the reconstruction of the Royal Castle at Warsaw.

To paraphrase Winston Churchill, the curtain was descending on eastern European dance shows at the Gardens as détente and cultural exchanges, not to mention Canada-Russia hockey games, were supplanted by international crises. Yet another era had passed.

There have been some interesting discussions and elegant arguments about dance in Maple Leaf Gardens. Critics have often spoken about the unsuitability of the building for ballet. One letter written to the *Globe and Mail* stated that the last Royal Ballet performance in the arena was a disgraceful comment on the state of North American theatre economics. But there is another, more positive side to the question of economics. The very size of the Gardens allowed Torontonians to see the famed Royal Ballet for as little as $3.00 per seat, whereas prices at the Metropolitan in New York ranged to $25.00. The Royal played an entire week at the Place des Arts in Montreal, took in $120,000 and lost money. The Gardens had no intention of losing money, nor did it expect to lose its position as the leader of cultural, artistic and sporting life in Canada. John Lanchberry, conductor of the Royal Ballet orchestra, once said, "What a splendid building this is," and despite the many critics it was the Gardens that was in the forefront of introducing the great dance companies to Toronto and to the nation.

MAPLE
LEAF
GARDENS
TORONTO PRICE CANADA
15¢

OFFICIAL PROGRAMME
JAN 21 1939

Official Programme

STANLEY CUP 1932

CHAMPIONS 1933

ALLAN CUP 1932

O.H.A. Jr. CHAMPS. S.P.A.

TORONTO MAPLE LEAFS

Price 15¢

MAPLE LEAF GARDENS
TORONTO - CANADA
JAN 8 - 1934

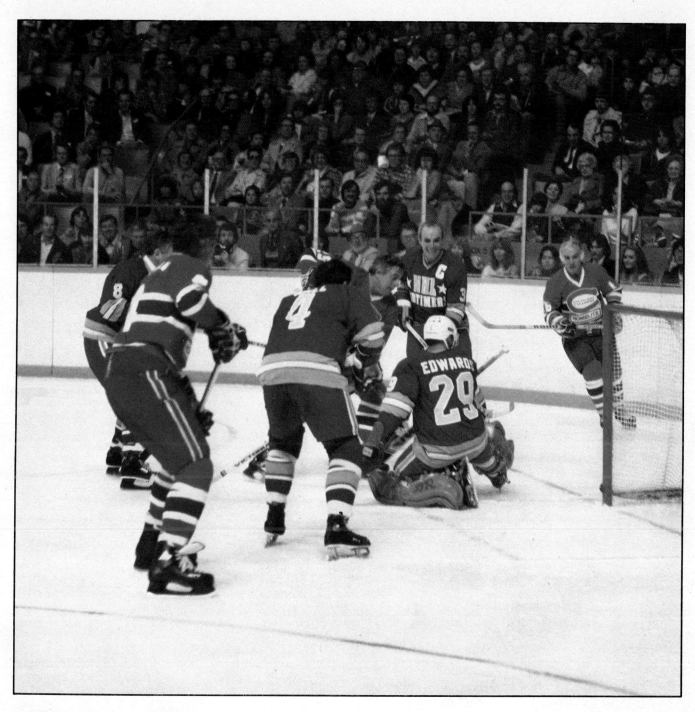

*A 1980 Old-Timers Game between
the Toronto Maple Leafs and the
Montreal Canadiens.*
JERRY HOBBS

*Syl Apps, a famous centre from the
30s and 40s.*

131

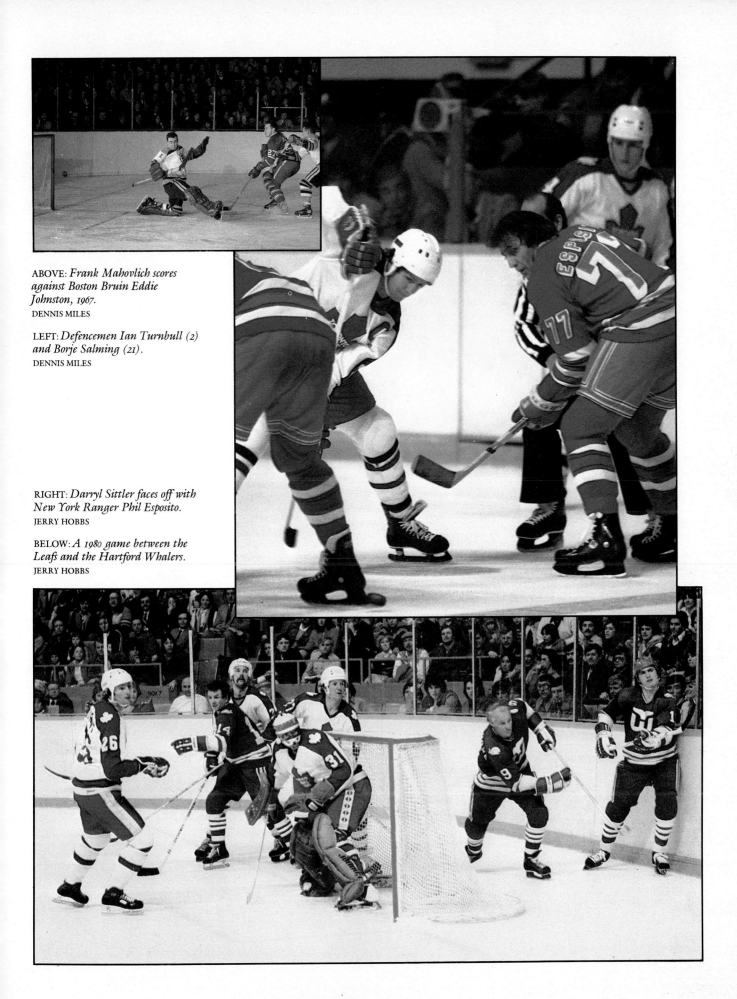

ABOVE: *Frank Mahovlich scores against Boston Bruin Eddie Johnston, 1967.*
DENNIS MILES

LEFT: *Defencemen Ian Turnbull (2) and Borje Salming (21).*
DENNIS MILES

RIGHT: *Darryl Sittler faces off with New York Ranger Phil Esposito.*
JERRY HOBBS

BELOW: *A 1980 game between the Leafs and the Hartford Whalers.*
JERRY HOBBS

Jiri Crha (31), Dave Burrows (behind) and Borje Salming (foreground) in a Leaf/Minnesota North Stars game, 1980.
DENNIS MILES

Leafs of the 60s: Allan Stanley (26), Tim Horton (7), goalie Johnnie Bower and Dave Keon (14).
DENNIS MILES

32-33

INDOOR LACROSSE

APR - 3 1933

MAPLE LEAF GARDENS

OFFICIAL PROGRAMME

TORONTO   PRICE 15¢   CANADA

Tennis at the Gardens, 1981.
JERRY HOBBS

Bjorn Borg at the 1981 Molson Challenge.
JERRY HOBBS

Vitas Gerulaitas won the 1981 Molson Challenge Cup.
JERRY HOBBS

Abby Hoffman.
DENNIS MILES

*Curly Neal of the Harlem
Globetrotters.*
DENNIS MILES

A gymnast at a Milk Meet.
DENNIS MILES

The 1945 Ice Capades.

Former Canadian champion, Lynn Nightingale, in a 1979 Ice Capades show.

A 1978 Garden Bros. Circus performance.

Barry Gibb of the Bee Gees.
PETER CORIGLIONE

Roger Daltry of The Who.
PETER CORIGLIONE

The Rolling Stones.
ASHLEY LUBIN

*Two great evangelists, Billy Graham
(third from right) and Charles
Templeton (second from right) at
the Gardens in 1946.*

CHAPTER IX   RELIGIOUS MEETINGS

HISTORIAN AND AUTHOR William Kilbourn has called Maple Leaf Gardens "the most famous religious building in Canada." At first glance this might seem an unusual statement until we come to look at the number and stature of religious figures that have passed through the building during its history. The central importance of the Gardens to religion in Canada was particularly evident between the 1930s and the 1950s. Admittedly, the interest in religious speakers and rallies waned somewhat after the late fifties, but it quickly picked up again and seems to be on the rise into the decade of the eighties.

Almost everyone who has gained prominence in either national or international religious circles has appeared at the Gardens to inspire the faithful, from Aimee Semple McPherson to the Archbishop of Canterbury to Billy Graham. The most notable exception is the Pope, although there are plans afoot to invite him should he make a trip to Canada in the near future.

Events of a religious nature were among the first to be held at the Gardens. The Maple Leafs had won their first Stanley Cup and Winston Churchill had passed through on his way to making history when Denton Massey, a member of the powerful Toronto family and brother to Raymond, the actor, and Vincent, a future Governor General, organized the York Bible Class in the building. Massey had previously been holding his meetings at various places in Toronto, but by May, 1932, his following had become so large that only the Gardens was capable of accommodating him and the 14,000 people who came to hear him speak.

As an example of Massey's popularity and the significance of religion at the beginning of the Depression, the first York Bible Class attracted a capacity crowd, and many people who could not get tickets were turned away. Denton enthusiastically led the throng in many old hymns, accompanied by the 48th Highlanders band and the Mendelssohn Choir, under the direction of Dr. H. A. Fricker.

As Winston Churchill did before him, Massey dispensed with the microphone and spoke directly to the crowd, his strong clear voice easily heard even in the highest seats. "The devil," he said, "is always seeking to find the vulnerable spot of a Christian's faith. To the Christian who is fully armoured by faith, the devil cannot penetrate his defences." Massey's stirring words were well received by those in the audience that night.

Judge J. F. Rutherford, the founder of the Jehovah's Witnesses, also spoke to assemblies in the building in 1934 and 1938. The Witnesses returned in the late 1940s and early 1950s as the Watch Tower Bible and Tract Society. Close on the heels of the Witnesses' first meeting at the Gardens came a Canadian who had established herself as one of the most important religious personages of the day — Aimee Semple McPherson. In September of 1934 she spoke at the Gardens to several thousand people who had come to hear her life story. The night was as much a show as a religious event. McPherson wore a gown of eggshell-coloured crepe, a cape with frilled cuffs lined with scarlet and a red-jewelled cross pendant around her neck. She lectured for over an hour as the Ukrainian Choir in native costume provided background music.

She held aloft a white-bound Bible in one hand and a textbook on evolution in the other and recalled her schooldays when evolution had been taught to her instead of the teachings of the Bible. She spoke of her marriage to young Robert Semple, their two years in China, her return to Canada as a widow, her work in Canada and the building of the Angelus Temple. There, she claimed, 34,000 people had been baptized by immersion over the past decade. She also discussed the dangers of modern life, illustrated by an example from the day before. Driving toward Toronto from Brampton at seventy miles per hour, she had the misfortune to blow a tire, but was able to safely stop the car. Divine Providence — or good driving?

At the end of the meeting hundreds rushed to the platform to shake her hand. In a last bit of showmanship, she scattered gladioli among the audience from a bouquet she had received before the show.

Yet another female religious figure came to the building and filled the seats for the lecture "The World's Greatest Romance." Many were moved to tears on October 6, 1935, as Salvation Army General Evangeline Booth told the story of the conversion of a sinner, "Brute Dan," the drunkard and gambler.

With world war looming, concern was being expressed in Canada over the plight of the Jews in Germany. To this end, nearly 17,000 people packed the Gardens late in November, 1938, while nearly 3,000 more met at other places in the city, in a rally sponsored by the Canadian Jewish Congress. The theme of the assembly was the need for solidarity among all races and creeds in order to preserve freedom of religious thought and expression. There were many important people in attendance at the Gardens, both Jewish and non-Jewish, all with the conviction that the right to religious belief was being threatened by the Nazis.

The Salvation Army's fifty-third Annual Congress, October 6, 1935.

A United Church of Canada celebration, 1945.
GLOBE AND MAIL

The onset of the war only heightened this feeling, and the Congress held another meeting in the building on September 8, 1943, to graphically illustrate the condition of Jews in Europe and enlist Canadian support for their cause. Two Russian Jews who had escaped to North America spoke in Yiddish to over 12,000 people, telling them that Jews on this continent must be steadfast against fascism in all its forms. The dramatic surrender of Italy lent an air of excitement to the crowd's reaction to these heroic speakers. The escapees finished by talking about Nazi horrors in Europe, and they were followed by other prominent Jews, including author Solomon Asch, who spoke out against Canada's policy of restricting Jewish immigration. It was a moving meeting, but unfortunately one that was not heeded seriously enough by the general populace. At the close of the rally, a recorded message of support was played from Albert Einstein, who was too ill to attend.

The war years saw a number of different religious groups at the Gardens such as the People's Church, youth rallies and at least one military church parade. Many of the soldiers considered it a bit of a lark to march to the Gardens in a church parade, knowing that they were practising religion in a building where hockey, wrestling and boxing had become almost like a religion to many in the city.

But participation at religious meetings did not die with the end of the war. On June 10, 1945, barely a month after V-E Day, nearly 20,000 people in the building and an overflow of 1,200 on Carlton Street heard the United Church membership of Toronto inaugurate a crusade whose theme was "Advancing for Christ and His Kingdom" on the twentieth anniversary of church union. The audience pledged to try and "win to Christ and His Church all these individuals and families in our own and other lands not yet reached by the gospel message." The pledge was led from the stage where there was a large, lighted cross backed by a massed choir of 1,200 voices, including guest soloist Portia White.

Aside from Separate School hockey tournaments and Board of Education meetings, the city's Roman Catholics made their first appearance at the Gardens in March of 1946. The reason was a public reception to honour the elevation of James Cardinal McGuigan, Archbishop of Toronto. His Eminence responded to the continuous cheers of his flock by waving his scarlet biretta as he walked between rows of Catholic war veterans. The newly installed cardinal took the opportunity to elevate eight Toronto archdiocese priests to the rank of monsignor.

The Gardens hosted a religious triumph on August 16, 1963. On this date the Anglican Congress was held there, the largest Anglican conference to be held anywhere in the world in this century. In attendance was Geoffrey Fisher, Archbishop of Canterbury.

The famed evangelist Aimee Semple McPherson at the Gardens in September, 1934.

The Catholics returned in 1963 and again on October 1, 1966, to observe Poland's millenium of Christianity, an event celebrated in many parts of the world. Poland's Communist regime had claimed that such celebrations were motivated by politics, but at a Mass held at St. Peter's in Rome earlier in the year Pope Paul VI asserted that the motivations were strictly religious. In Toronto, the Pope was represented by his personal delegate, Stefan Cardinal Wyszinski, Primate of Poland, and the principal celebrant of the Mass was Ladislaus Rubin (now a Cardinal), Delegate for the Polish Refugees in Exile.

Another segment of the religious community was represented by one of the best-loved evangelists of all time. Billy Graham made his fifth trip to the Gardens in 1980, nearly thirty-five years after he had first visited the building in 1946 to speak at a Youth for Christ rally. Charles Templeton, evangelist then and author now, also appeared on stage with Graham during this first visit, as did Mayor Bob Saunders of Toronto. Graham returned in 1955 for another rally, and in 1956 he spoke at the Greater Evangelistic Crusade of Toronto.

One of his greatest moments was in June, 1978, when the Billy Graham Crusade was held at the Gardens. Eighteen thousand people packed the building, while an additional 8,000 stood outside. Despite criticism of his style by some local clergymen, Graham was able to convert more than 6,000 people during his four-day visit. Celebrities abounded, such as singer Robert Goulet and hockey stars Paul Henderson and Ron Ellis.

Even those who couldn't get into the building past the watchful ushers weren't completely disappointed. Graham made a brief appearance outside to console the crowd, gave a short synopsis of his address inside and asked those who wanted to be saved to raise their hands. Hundreds responded, and they were asked to return to one of the other meetings. Even after this, hundreds more remained on the sidewalk until after the meeting was over.

Undoubtedly one of the largest religious gatherings ever to take place at the Gardens, and the last before the building passed its fiftieth anniversary, was the Baptist World Congress of 1980. Billy Graham attended as a speaker, and the list of dignitaries from all over the world was long and impressive. The congress marked the seventy-fifth anniversary of the Baptist World Alliance, and 20,000 faithful jammed the Gardens and every hotel in the downtown area. Speakers such as Noel Vose from Australia, William A. Jones, Jr. from the United States, Lien Chow from Taiwan, Edwin Lopez of the Philippines and S. T. Oba Akande of Nigeria kept the crowd enthralled through the sweltering June heat. It was rumoured that President Jimmy Carter would also attend, but various political problems forced him to cancel whatever plans may have been made.

OPPOSITE, TOP: *On June 11, 1978, 17,000 people jammed the Gardens to hear Billy Graham.*
TORONTO SUN

OPPOSITE, BOTTOM: *Youth for Christ rally, June 16, 1945.*

This brief account of religious highlights and eminent religious figures at the Gardens cannot hope to cover every event of a like nature. For example, the Greek Community of Toronto held an annual service there from 1964 to 1970, the Canadian Council of Churches has met in the building, there was a World Convention of Churches of Christ, a Ukrainian church service and an area conference of the Church of Latter Day Saints. The Gardens has been a focal point for religious activities on a grand scale over the past half-century and will undoubtedly remain so as the building enters its second fifty years.

Eucharistic Diocesan Mass, June 1, 1963.
GRAPHIC ARTISTS

The stage and choir, United Church of Canada celebration, 1945.
GLOBE AND MAIL

Winston Churchill waving to the crowd in 1932 before entering the Gardens for his lecture.
TORONTO STAR

CHAPTER X POLITICIANS AND ROYALTY

IF YOU'VE EVER BEEN ANYONE in Canadian political life, you've been on stage at Maple Leaf Gardens. On a federal level, the building has been involved in every election since 1949, and not a few before that. William Lyon Mackenzie King, Louis St. Laurent, Lester Pearson, Joe Clark, Pierre Trudeau, Robert Stanfield and John Diefenbaker have had their day. On a local and provincial level, politicians like David Crombie and William Davis have spoken and been entertained under the same roof as such international figures as Winston Churchill, Wendell Wilkie and Robert Kennedy. Canada's close ties to the British monarchy have led to several gracious royal visits, while the ruling princes and princesses of other lands have also found the time to appear at Church and Carlton streets.

Premier George S. Henry of Ontario and Mayor William Stewart of Toronto were on hand to help open the building on November 12, 1931, so it might be said that politicians got into the act even before the first audience took their seats. But the first politician of international stature to appear at the Gardens was Winston Churchill who lectured to 6,000 people on "British Imperialism." The date was March 3, 1932.

Churchill was on a North American tour, and he arrived in Toronto by train accompanied by his daughter, Diana. Shortly before his death, Conn Smythe was asked whether he had met the great man, and he replied, "No. Churchill spent all his time at Bickell's [J. P. Bickell, first President of the Gardens] drinking the cellar dry." It was left to Arthur Meighen, former Prime Minister of Canada, to introduce the famous lecturer to the Gardens' crowd once he had entered the building to the strains of "Rule Britannia."

The audience was expectant, but the great man wasn't quite ready. He had come to favour the lapel microphones he had used on earlier tour stops, and Foster Hewitt recalled that Churchill asked for one on this occasion. Hewitt warned that a lapel microphone couldn't cope with the thirteen-and-a-half second echo lapse in the building, but Churchill would have his way.

"Young man, when I want your advice, I'll ask for it," Churchill responded. In desperation, Hewitt set up a floor microphone, but

Churchill knocked it over. "Can you hear me?" Churchill asked the crowd. "No!" came the resounding reply. The lecturer dispensed with microphones entirely, explaining, "I take no responsibility for the technical arrangements. But the resources of civilization being exhausted, I will do the best I can on my own."

Churchill spoke for an hour without the aid of "the resources of civilization," and predictably the size of the arena gave him a hard time. Foster Hewitt remembered that, "Winston didn't make himself heard to a lot of people. It was probably one of the few times in history that he didn't get his point across." Nevertheless, the *Globe* reported, "Mr. Churchill's best was good enough, as a contented silence fell upon the Gardens."

Churchill must have sensed that war was coming, because the entire lecture centred on the need for a strong Commonwealth. "Mark you," he said, "England's weakness is the world's danger, and the strength of the Empire is the world's peace." Churchill said many things that night, but nothing so emphatically. This premonition marked in a way the beginning of his ascent to political power and historical importance.

On the opposite end of the political spectrum, Tim Buck, Canada's best known Communist, obtained permission to speak at the Gardens on December 2, 1934. Over 17,000 people turned out to welcome this man who had just been released from the Kingston Penitentiary. The fact that the audience was almost three times the size of the one that attended the Churchill lecture was a direct reflection of public concern about national and international political events of the day. It is easy to see in hindsight that Churchill's warnings were the most telling, but at the time Buck's appeal to the common man was more immediate.

Buck was one of the original members of the Communist Party in Canada. He was born in England, emigrating in 1910. After attending the Lenin School in Moscow, he returned to Canada and assumed the party leadership. Buck was arrested in 1931 under terms of Section 98 of the Criminal Code, a statute that effectively banned Communism. He and six of his most important lieutenants were carted off to jail. As a result, the party worked tirelessly for his release under the direction of former Methodist minister A. E. Smith. In the autumn of 1932, prisoners rioted at the Kingston jail, and even though Buck was not part of the disturbance, nor was his cell near the trouble spot, some guards felt that he was responsible. They went to his cell and fired into it with pistols and shotguns. Inquiries in the House of Commons never established why they fired, or why they missed.

Buck and the other Communist prisoners were finally released in 1934 after a petition bearing 20,000 signatures was effective in repealing Section 98. Buck's was a hero's return, and he was met at Toronto's Union Station by 4,000 supporters who carried him on their shoulders

to the Gardens. There, Buck recounted the history of his imprison-
ment, extolled the virtues of the Communist Party and dared the
government to jail him again.

With sabre-rattling in Europe, the Depression draining the country
and a federal election looming, attention was diverted from Buck's
cause during the following year. In late 1935, there were three election
rallies held in the building which were the largest ever held in Canada.
The Liberals were first to move into the Gardens, and on October 8,
1935 a capacity crowd heard Mackenzie King shout his slogan, "It's
King or Chaos." Support for King was widespread, and eight provincial premiers sent their best wishes "by the wireless." An hour before
the meeting commenced, three separate crowds were storming the
Gardens' entrances. The queue at the main door was twelve deep and
stretched half-way to Yonge Street. Police on foot and horseback had a
difficult time trying to guide the crowd as it moved "like stampeding
steers" toward the turnstiles.

One of the speakers at the rally was Lionel Conacher, football and
hockey star. He told the audience that while he had been in the
Gardens many times, he had never been asked to speak on the same
platform as the next prime minister. Predictably, this comment drew a
round of cheers, but it was suggested that at least some of the spectators came only to see the man who would later be named Canada's
athlete of the half-century.

The following night, October 9, 1935, the Conservatives, under
Prime Minister R. B. Bennett, took over the building. Mackenzie King's
oration must have still been ringing in the rafters, or perhaps Bennett
knew that he had led the country through five difficult Depression
years, and it would take a superhuman effort to get re-elected. Nevertheless, Bennett invited all "commoners" to return the Conservatives
to power, stating that he would lead them without regard for party
and would settle their economic problems. Both of these were glow-
ing promises that would be difficult to fulfill in the depths of the
Great Depression. Bennett also warned that Ontario Liberal premier
Mitchell Hepburn was on the road to ruining the province, yet another
reason why the Tories should be in office. Bennett spoke before 15,000
wildly cheering people at the Gardens, and the audience was swelled
considerably by the relatively new feature of a nation-wide radio
broadcast.

For the third time in four days, another political gathering was held,
this time on October 11. The Hon. Harry H. Stevens and his Reconstruction Party attracted a crowd of 10,000 supporters. Stevens was the
former Minister of Trade in the Bennett government, but he had quit
his post after embarrassing the government in 1934 with a probe into
price spreads. The new party was formed, therefore, "to get a better
deal for the little man."

As the two previous meetings had hailed their respective leaders, the Reconstruction rally touted Stevens as the next Prime Minister of Canada. His ninety-minute speech upheld the party platform as he promised a new and better financial system for Canada where "sweat-shops would be smashed and consumers protected" and British capital would be invested in the nation. This was by far the largest rally in Stevens' whirlwind tour of Canada, and the size of the audience points out just how concerned Canadian voters were about the state of the economy.

Mackenzie King packed the Gardens to the roof, Bennett's meeting was short of that, while Stevens' was even smaller. Enthusiasm, of course, was high at all three meetings, but of the three leaders, only King spoke without being heckled. The election went the way of the Gardens' attendance. The Liberals swept the country with 171 seats to the Conservatives' thirty-nine. The only Reconstruction Party member to be elected was H. H. Stevens, and the party was soon to collapse.

King may have won the election, but the Conservatives weren't through with him yet. In March of 1940, R. J. Manion, Ontario Conservative leader, addressed nearly 16,000 people at the Gardens, and his message was that everyone in Canada wanted unity in the war effort, except for one man, Mackenzie King. Amidst thundering cheers and rounds of applause, Manion asked the vast audience, "Has Mr. King got the sixteen best brains in Canada in his Cabinet?" A raucous "No!" from the crowd set the tone for the entire meeting.

The first American politician to address a Gardens' crowd was also concerned with the war. Wendell Wilkie spoke at a meeting of the Canadian War Services Fund on March 24, 1941. Although he had run unsuccessfully against Franklin D. Roosevelt in the presidential election, Wilkie's oratorical skills remained legendary, and Roosevelt was astute enough to make use of him during the war years as a goodwill ambassador.

After dining at the York Club with Mackenzie King, Wilkie came to Church and Carlton completely carried away with enthusiasm for the cause he was pleading. He called for Canada and the United States to supply Britain with every ship she needed, so that the beleaguered island could turn full attention to building planes. The audience was a large one, and after Wilkie took off his glasses and threw away his prepared speech, nearly every sentence of his ad libbed, eloquent plea was met with thundering applause.

King and Mitchell Hepburn joined Wilkie on stage and expressed their support of his views. More than $7,000 was raised from meeting tickets, and Wilkie presented King with a cheque for $22,500 from the Linen Trade Association in the United States to be used for buying a Spitfire fighter plane.

Communist leader Tim Buck (left) at the October 13, 1942, meeting of the Communist Labour and Total War Committee.
ALEXANDRA STUDIO

The war brought yet another American politician to the Gardens. Dorothy Thompson, a journalist who many thought would be the first woman President of the United States, came to Toronto just three months after Wilkie. She entered the building behind the St. Mary's Boys Band and three steel-helmeted soldiers carrying the Union Jack followed by three members of the Red Cross Corps waving the Stars and Stripes. Miss Thompson addressed a crowd of 18,000 at a Women's Victory Loan rally, and she called for the women of Canada to "end this gothic madness" and to "fight for a world in which we can live." It was a thrilling and inspiring pageant in support of the war effort, but Canada was not yet ready for Thompson's feminist message.

A Canadian politician and suffragette, Doris Neilson M.P., also appeared at the Gardens during the same year in support of the war. The meeting was held under the auspices of the *Canadian Tribune*, and Neilson spoke along with Leslie Roberts and A. A. MacLeod. Roberts was later to become a prominent radio broadcaster in Montreal, while Doris Neilson moved to China once her political career ended, where she died in late 1980.

October 13, 1942 saw a meeting of strange bedfellows. Ignoring all differences in a concerted effort to achieve national unity, leaders of political groups, labour bodies and church organizations joined with the Communists on the stage of Maple Leaf Gardens to demand that the ban on the Communist Party be lifted. The fact that only 9,000 people showed up, rather than the 13,000 expected, was probably a result of the high employment percentages reached during the war and an indication that many people were not yet ready for, or no longer interested in, radical politics. Even though politicians and the major figures in Canadian Communism were there, not even Tim Buck, Leopold Macaulay or Mitchell Hepburn could fill the building. This was the last large Communist Party rally held in Canada.

The war was still the most important topic for speakers at the Gardens, and the question of relations with Russia was a major theme. Wendell Wilkie returned to the building in 1942 to take part in an Aid for Russia rally, one of many during this period. A highlight of the 1942 meeting was the revelation that the national chairman of the Aid to Russia Committee and five of his friends had personally donated $50,000 to the cause. Wilkie told the crowd of 7,500 that the democracies had to work with Russia in both war and peace. He went on to say that the best response to the threat posed by Communism "is a living, vibrant, fearless democracy — economic, social and political." As the war wound down, however, it became increasingly apparent that Russia was more an enemy than a friend. With the Allies in control of the fighting, these Aid to Russia benefits ended.

So great was the crowd waiting to get into the Gardens for the 1935 Liberal rally that the mounted police were called in to keep order.
ALEXANDRA STUDIO

LEFT: *Wendell Wilkie addressing a Gardens' crowd during the war.*
ALEXANDRA STUDIO

RIGHT: *Dorothy Thompson (holding bouquet) prepares to speak to a Gardens' audience on June 3, 1941.*
ALEXANDRA STUDIO

Prime Minister Louis St. Laurent and his wife arrive at the Gardens for a Liberal Party rally, August, 1953.
ALEXANDRA STUDIO

Doris Neilson, M.P. for North Battleford, signs autographs before a meeting of the Canadian Seamen's Union on December 6, 1940.
ALEXANDRA STUDIO

In Canadian politics, Mackenzie King resigned, and Louis St. Laurent took over the Liberal helm. The Liberals held rallies at the Gardens every election year from 1949 to 1957, and the 1949 meeting revealed St. Laurent both as a politician and as a man. The Prime Minister arrived in Toronto on a wave of popularity. Wherever his campaign train had halted in southwestern Ontario record crowds were there to greet him. It was estimated that three million Canadians had heard him speak during the nearly twelve thousand miles of his campaign trip.

St. Laurent told the crowd at the triumphal rally that his friends were correct when they told him that although he knew something about law (he was a lawyer after all), he knew nothing about politics. "They're right," he told the 13,500 supporters, "I know nothing about a certain kind of politics." This brought hundreds to the platform to shake his hand once he had finished speaking.

St. Laurent endeared himself to the audience because he was a man whose brilliance of mind was matched by his kindness of heart. His strongest point was that he told the truth, and his campaign used this honesty as a central issue. "In other words, the truth and nothing but the truth," he said. "At the bar I found that was a pretty successful system, and when I did go to this other forum, I laid my case before the public."

St. Laurent's political career was long and illustrious, and the Gardens was fortunate to have him and other political leaders of such stature appear beneath its roof. His last public appearance in the building occurred on October 14, 1961, shortly before his death, when he dropped the puck for the opening of the hockey season.

Political leaders have not always come to Maple Leaf Gardens to plead a cause or further election hopes. Another famous American politician came to the building, this time in the 1960s, but the circumstances were certainly different than on previous occasions. At nine o'clock one evening, a long-haired man entered the Hot Stove Club, and he was met and stopped at the door by the assistant manager. The man turned out to be Senator Robert Kennedy.

The astonished assistant manager later told reporters, "How could I know? He was alone, he was an hour late, and . . . he had long hair!"

Despite this unusual incident, political figures have a long tradition of attending Leafs' hockey games at the Gardens. Canadian prime ministers have often been spectators. Lester Pearson, for example, had a habit of showing up at the last minute, causing a scramble to find a suitable seat. Both Pierre Elliott Trudeau and Joe Clark have been in the crowd, and John Diefenbaker opened the hockey season in 1959.

Diefenbaker was a fiery orator, and he had been on the Gardens' stage the year before this opening ceremony to address the World Baptist Youth Conference. Even though he had a remarkable ability to sway a crowd, the low point of his political career came during the 1967 Progressive Conservative convention, when he was unceremoniously dumped as leader and replaced by Robert Stanfield.

The weather was hot in Toronto the night of the convention, and the delegates decided to take a break from the long round of meetings. The Gardens sent out for fruit from its regular supplier, "Banana Joe" Lamantia, who was also the penalty timekeeper for Leafs' games. Stanfield wanted a banana, the photographers got into the act and an image was born. For a long time thereafter Stanfield was cartooned with a banana as the main prop.

Cartoons aside, this was one of the most dramatic conventions ever held in the building. Previous candidates for that distinction were the two held by the New Democratic Party in 1963 and 1965, especially the latter, where Tommy Douglas made an impassioned plea for the return of American soldiers from Viet Nam. But the 1967 convention was magnificent theatre. Organized by Eddie Goodman, it was attended by such powerful political figures as Mike Starr, Wallace McCutcheon, Davie Fulton, and, of course, John Diefenbaker. There was talk of *Deux Nations*, and voting machines were rented from the Liberals. In the end, however, with Trudeaumania sweeping the country, the Conservatives fared badly in the election, regardless of the show they put on at the Gardens.

For pure theatre, the Liberals were hard to beat. Their 1972 convention was organized with an eye on the fact that the rock and roll generation had become a significant voting block. Trudeaumania was still going strong, and the Liberals staged a show featuring the Optimist Band, Crowbar and The Travellers. Trudeau, it seemed, merely had to show up to be re-elected.

Trudeau has been a fairly regular face at the Gardens. After the 1972 convention, he returned for the Ontario Invitational Floor Hockey Tournament for the Mentally Retarded in 1974, various track meets and hockey games, the Liberal Party convention in 1979 and the Molson Challenge Cup tennis tournament in 1981.

The Liberal convention of May 9, 1979, was a throwback to the 1972 convention, with performers and rock music filling the ears of the 20,000 people who packed the building in sweltering heart. No one smoked dope or tossed frisbees, but as one usher commented, "It's too loud for these people. The old can't take it." This statement alone was indicative of the type of crowd that was attracted, but which was obviously far different from the 1972 gathering.

It was possibly a comment on the age of the people in attendance, or the age of the centre of attraction, Pierre Elliott Trudeau, but in any case the Downchild Blues Band belted it out, dedicating one tune to "our favourite PET, and it's called TV Mama." This reference must have been lost on many in the crowd who could hardly hear anymore,

Prime Minister Pierre Trudeau, who has attended numerous events and rallies at the Gardens, chats with Gardens' President Harold Ballard on May 9, 1979.
JOHN MAIOLA

much less think about jokes. Sylvia Tyson performed, but when the Good Brothers performed "The Orange Blossom Special," the crowd started to chant "Trudeau! Trudeau! Trudeau!" Three hours after the concert began, the star appeared.

Liberal fortunes were markedly on the decline by this time, and the mood of the rally certainly did not accurately reflect the feelings of a country fighting inflation and high unemployment. The Liberals were swept from office at the next federal election, and this was the last of the great political conventions held at the Gardens up to the present.

It is difficult to walk through the Gardens today and not still hear echoes of the great political speakers who have stated their points of view and have left their political futures in the hands of the electorate. Their fortunes and our fortunes have been closely tied to events under the Gardens' roof.

The influence of royalty has been consistently felt at the Gardens over the years, just as it has been in Canada as a whole. Many royal figures, from the present Queen of England, to Nordic and Asiatic princes and princesses have visited the building at one time or another.

An unprecedented event in Gardens' history took place on January 21, 1936. The Maple Leafs were scheduled to play the Montreal Canadiens, but to commemorate the death of King George V the game was cancelled and rescheduled. So strong was the admiration for the King that in addition to the cancellation a memorial service was held a few days later. A similar cancellation and memorial service took place with the death of King George VI. Only three hockey games have ever been cancelled in the building, these two and another when Stafford Smythe passed away.

British royalty first visited the building on October 13, 1951. Her Royal Highness Princess Elizabeth, who was to become Queen Elizabeth when George VI died the following year, came with her husband, Prince Philip, to see a hockey game as part of their Canadian tour. The Chicago Black Hawks and the Maple Leafs played a special abbreviated game for them at 3:00 p.m., and the same teams played a regular game that evening to launch the new season. Conn Smythe presented the Princess with the game puck and told her that it was for Prince Charles, whom the Leafs were putting on their negotiation list.

Yet it was another son, Prince Andrew, who caused the most stir in the building, even though he wasn't on a negotiation list. In 1977, when the Maple Leafs were celebrating their fiftieth anniversary, the young Prince visited the Gardens, and Harold Ballard took him on a tour of the team's dressing room during an intermission of a Toronto-Buffalo game. The irrepressible Tiger Williams, who now plays with Vancouver, broke decorum and shouted, "Hi, Andy!" Harold Ballard continued in this informal vein and said, "Young man,

In the royal box with Conn Smythe,
Princess Elizabeth accepts a bouquet
from an admirer.
ALEXANDRA STUDIO

Prince Andrew took in a Leaf game
in 1977 and visited the dressing room
between periods. He is shown here
shaking hands with Darryl Sittler.
Coach Red Kelly (beside Prince
Andrew), trainer Dan Lemelin and
the author are in the background.
TORONTO SUN

I remember when your father was here for a game." Prince Andrew returned twice more, but incognito, in order to attend rock concerts. He still wasn't put on the negotiation list, though.

When His Royal Highness Prince Bertil of Sweden came to the Gardens in November of 1966, he was able to appreciate the hockey game he saw, because in his youth he had been a champion speed-skater. The Prince was kind enough to appear on television between the first and second periods, and he spoke warmly of the game.

To help celebrate Canada's Centennial in 1967, Princess Alexandra of Kent was gracious enough to attend the Ontario Folk Arts Festival held at the Gardens on May 16. While her visit was certainly pleasant for all concerned, the arrival of Prince Bernhard of the Netherlands in 1972 did cause some commotion. He and his twenty-two person retinue were to attend a hockey game on February 23, and a list of preferred foods was submitted to the Hot Stove Club where they were to dine before the opening face-off. Only Iranian caviar was to be served, no German wines, no thickened soups, no ice cream. The royal party had just been seated for dinner when it was announced that the game had started. Without a word, the Prince arose, followed by his entire entourage, and left to watch the game. Coach John McLellan was ill that evening, so King Clancy took over behind the bench. Someone in the royal party observed, "Your Royal Highness, there is a king coaching this team."

Among the members of several Asiatic royal families who have graced the Gardens, Prince Yusef and Princess Norain of Burnei (formerly Borneo) possibly came the greatest distance. They had flown half-way round the world to bring their two-year-old daughter for treatment at Toronto's Hospital for Sick Children. The mission was anxious, though happily successful, and they were able to spare the time to attend an Ice Follies performance on January 22, 1980. In a fitting tribute, Richard Dwyer, who distributes roses among the crowd during these performances, presented them to Princess Norain as a memento of her visit.

It is satisfying to look back and know that even royalty, like so many other people during the long history of the Gardens, have been able to find a moment's comfort and enjoyment under the roof of the grand old building on Carlton Street.

Boxing match between Young Stribling and Joe Doctor, 1932.
PRINGLE & BOOTH LIMITED

Sonja Henie, 1938.
ALEXANDRA STUDIO

King Clancy (left) and Conn Smythe.

Team photo for the Ace Bailey benefit, 1934.
ALEXANDRA STUDIO

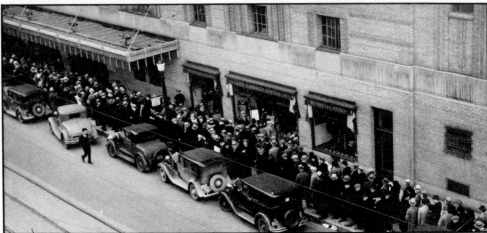

Lining up for tickets.
PRINGLE & BOOTH LIMITED

CHRONOLOGY

Listed here year by year are many of the significant events in the history of Maple Leaf Gardens. All the boxing and wrestling matches, the hockey games, the bingos and other charitable or community events, the annual appearances by groups as diverse as the Harlem Globetrotters and the Toronto Police Association that have taken place over fifty years cannot be listed, but the following chronology, developed with the help of Nancy Ryder, Gord Finn and Irwin "Patty" Patoff, records the highlights, records and firsts.

1931

NOVEMBER 12: Maple Leaf Gardens opens in the middle of the Depression with a hockey game between the Chicago Black Hawks and the Toronto Maple Leafs. Mayor W. J. Stewart dropped the first puck, and Ace Bailey took the first face-off for the Leafs. The Black Hawks won the game 2-1, the first goal in the Gardens scored by Mush March of Chicago, the first Toronto goal by Charlie Conacher. Vic Ripley scored the other Chicago goal.

NOVEMBER 13: The first Ontario Hockey Association senior game was played, with the Nationals beating the Marlboros 3-2.

NOVEMBER 16: The first junior games at the Gardens were played in the SPA league. Toronto Canoe Club beat University of Toronto Schools 10-0. Harry Neale had the first shut-out in the building. Aurora and West Toronto played in the second half of the doubleheader.

NOVEMBER 17: Marlboros beat Hamilton 6-0. This was the Marlies' first shut-out in the building, recorded by Phil Stein, later a goalie with the Leafs.

NOVEMBER 19: The Queensbury Athletic Club held its first wrestling match in the new building, drawing 15,300 persons for a four-fight card. Jim Londos beat Gino Garibaldi in the main event.

NOVEMBER 28: Leafs beat Boston 4-3, the first victory for the Leafs in the new building.

DECEMBER 6: Leafs beat the Montreal Maroons 4-0, the first Leaf shut-out in the Gardens. Lorne Chabot was in the nets for Toronto.

1932

FEBRUARY 6: Charlie Conacher scores the fastest opening goal in seven seconds, a club record. Toronto 6, Boston 0.

MARCH 3: Winston Churchill lectures, introduced by Arthur Meighen.

APRIL 9: Toronto Maple Leafs win the third game of a best-of-five series to capture the Stanley Cup, the first of eleven up to 1981, with a 6-4 win over the Rangers. The men on that team included Lorne Chabot, Red Horner, Alex Levinsky, Andy Blair, Ace Bailey, Baldy Cotton, Busher Jackson, Frank Finnigan, Bob Gracie, Earl Miller, Harold Darragh, Fred Robertson, Hap Day, Charlie Conacher, King Clancy and Joe Primeau. The manager was Conn Smythe and the coach was Dick Irvin.

MAY 1: Denton Massey held his third and last meeting of the York Bible Class.

MAY 2: First Lions Club boxing show, for interprovincial championships, with Lou Marsh as referee. Montreal boxers won five of seven bouts.

MAY 3: Opening game of the International Lacrosse League. Maple Leafs defeated Tecumsehs 12-5.

MAY 4: First professional badminton challenge games. Jack Purcell and C. Aikman defeated J. Devlin and W. Jones.

MAY 12-13: Olympic boxing exhibition series.

MAY 19: World championship boxing. "Panama" Al Brown defeated "Spider" Pladner. This was the first world championship fight at the Gardens.

OCTOBER 21: First game of the Mann Cup lacrosse playoffs. Mimico Mountaineers defeated Winnipeg Argos 16-6.

OCTOBER 24: Mann Cup lacrosse final. Mimico Mountaineers defeated Winnipeg Argos 4-2 to take the Cup.

NOVEMBER 10: Opening game of the 1932-33 NHL Leaf schedule. Boston and Toronto tied 1-1. Hon. H. A. Bruce, Lieutenant-Governor of Ontario, dropped the puck.

1933

JANUARY 21: Benefit game between the Leafs and four senior OHA clubs: Niagara Falls, Toronto Nationals, Toronto Marlboros, University of Toronto. Leafs won all four games.

FEBRUARY 7: Public skating. The crowd was able to listen to the Leaf-Canadiens game broadcast by Foster Hewitt. Admission was 35 cents.

APRIL 3: Bill Tilden featured in a touring tennis match against Wimbledon champion Ellsworth Vines, the first tennis to be played in the building.

MAY 5: The Jehovah's Witnesses, with Judge Rutherford.

NOVEMBER 6: Hap Day's and King Clancy's "Newlyweds" played Ace Bailey's "Simon Pures" in a pre-season exhibition game. Simon Pures won 7-4.

NOVEMBER 9: Leafs' season opener. Toronto 6, Boston 1. Hon. H. A. Bruce,

Lieutenant-Governor of Ontario, dropped the opening puck.

DECEMBER 7: The annual game between the Upper Canada College Old Boys and the team of the day. Old Boys won 11-8.

DECEMBER 21: Queensbury Athletic Club Wrestling: George Zaharias versus Jim Browning. Browning won.

1934

JANUARY 11: Queensbury Athletic Club wrestling: Jim Londos versus Rudy Dusek. Londos won.

FEBRUARY 6-7: First North American speed-skating championships at the Gardens, sponsored by the Kiwanis Club.

FEBRUARY 14: Because of Ace Bailey's near-death in a hockey game at Boston, a benefit game was played for him, with the Leafs against the NHL All Stars. From this beginning, the All Star game became an annual event. Toronto beat the All Stars 7-3. A capacity crowd of 14,074 paid a total of $20,909.40 to see the game.

MARCH 31: First Allan Cup hockey final in the building. Moncton Hawks defeated the Fort William Thundering Herd 3-2 in the opening game.

APRIL 7: First international hockey game in the building. The United States, represented by the Detroit White Stars, defeated the Canadian champion Moncton Hawks 2-1 in overtime.

APRIL 27: Independent Order of Foresters (IOF) pageant. The Lilies of the Empire celebrated Toronto's Centennial.

APRIL 28: Toronto Girl Guides rally, celebrating the city's Centennial.

MAY 15-16: Catholic School Board pageant, celebrating Toronto's Centennial.

MAY 21-22: Dominion boxing championships.

MAY 24: Boy Scout pageant, celebrating Toronto's Centennial.

JUNE 9: Maple Leaf Athletic Club wrestling: Vic Christie versus The Masked Marvel. The Masked Marvel won.

JULY 8: The Jehovah's Witnesses, with Judge Rutherford.

SEPTEMBER 7: Aimee Semple McPherson gave a religious lecture.

SEPTEMBER 19: Oddfellows convention.

SEPTEMBER 21: Dancing with Eddie Duchin and his band.

OCTOBER 18: Queensbury Athletic Club wrestling: Earl McCready, Canadian Heavyweight Wrestling Champion, defeated Rudy Dusek in one fall.

OCTOBER 21-27: First of the six-day bicycle races, starring the Peden brothers, Torchy and Doug. Admission was 25 cents for the entire day.

NOVEMBER 8: Opening Leaf game. Toronto 5, Boston 3.

NOVEMBER 10: First NHL penalty shot at the Gardens, Leafs against Canadiens. Mondou of Montreal took the shot against Hainsworth of Toronto, but missed. Toronto won the game 2-1.

NOVEMBER 20: Harvey (Busher) Jackson set a Leaf NHL record with four goals in one period. Leafs beat St. Louis Eagles 5-2.

DECEMBER 2: Toronto and district labour forum. Communist leader Tim Buck spoke.

DECEMBER 22: First Young Canada Night. On a first-come basis, children could get into the hockey game free. Leafs played Chicago this night.

DECEMBER 31: New Year's Eve dance, with Don Retman's New York orchestra.

1935

Floodlighting was installed in the Gardens during this year.

MARCH 5: Toronto inter-religious church service.

MARCH 22: Maple Leaf Athletic Games. This was the first track meet at the building. Glenn Cunningham of Kansas was the featured miler.

APRIL 19: Professional tennis tournament, with Bill Tilden, Ellsworth Vines, George Lott and

Hans Neussel. Prices were $2.00, $1.50, $1.00 and 50 cents. Vines beat Tilden, and Vines and Tilden defeated Lott and Neussel in a doubles match.

SEPTEMBER 22-28: Six-day bicycle races.

OCTOBER 5: Admiral Richard Byrd, the great Antarctic explorer, lectured and showed his films.

OCTOBER 6: Salvation Army meeting, with Evangeline Booth.

OCTOBER 8: Liberal Party election rally, with Mackenzie King as the chief speaker.

OCTOBER 9: Conservative Party election rally, with Prime Minister R. B. Bennett as chief speaker.

OCTOBER 11: Reconstruction Party election rally, with Harry H. Stevens.

OCTOBER 12: Win Barron held a public meeting with five celebrities in an attempt to help the country through the Depression.

OCTOBER 25-26: Reginald Stewart Symphony Orchestra and the Radio City Ballet. This was the first time that ballet was staged at the Gardens.

OCTOBER 28-NOVEMBER 2: Bob Morton's Rameses Shrine Circus, the first circus in the building, was held annually in October until 1960.

NOVEMBER 9: NHL opener for Leafs, with Toronto and New York Americans playing to a 5-5 tie. The puck was dropped by the auto industrialist R. S. McLaughlin of Oshawa.

NOVEMBER 13: Boxing. Joe Louis, the great American boxing champion, appeared in an exhibition against four sparring partners and beat them all.

NOVEMBER 27: Five Pianos Ensemble: Alberto Guerrero, Reginald Godden, Scott Malcolm, Ernest Seitz, Reginald Stewart.

1936

Penalty clocks, designed by building superintendent Doug Morris, were installed during 1936.

JANUARY 7: The Canadian Olympic hockey team lost 4-3 to the Toronto Dukes. Tickets were priced at $1.15, 60 cents and 30 cents. This Canadian team was on its way to Germany to play for the world Olympic title, where it was defeated by a British team made up of Canadians born in England. Adolph Hitler presented the championship medals.

JANUARY 21: Game between the Montreal Canadiens and the Toronto Maple Leafs cancelled due to the death of King George V.

JANUARY 28: Memorial service for His Majesty King George V.

FEBRUARY 19: Jack Dempsey's heavyweight elimination boxing tournament. Red Munroe took four bouts and was crowned the White Hope Champion of Canada.

FEBRUARY 20: Postponed game of January 7 was played.

MARCH 20: Maple Leaf track meet: Achilles Club.

APRIL 13: Memorial Cup junior hockey: Saskatoon Wesleys lose to West Toronto 4-2, as the eastern team wins the championship.

APRIL 22: Queensbury Athletic Club White Hope boxing tournament.

APRIL 24: IOF pageant.

APRIL 27-MAY 2: Six-day bicycle race. The building opened at 12:30 a.m. This was the latest start of an event at the Gardens until a Frank Sinatra midnight show in the 1970s.

MAY 18: Olympic trials for amateur boxing. The event set off a wave of interest in boxing for the next few years in Toronto.

MAY 22: Apex Athletic Club's Double White Hope boxing tournament.

AUGUST 2: National model aircraft contest.

OCTOBER 2: Mann Cup lacrosse final: Orillia Terriers defeated Vancouver North Shore Indians 10-8.

OCTOBER 14: Opening of the Canadian Grand Opera season, with *Aida*.

OCTOBER 18: Federation for Community Service. The Toronto Symphony Orchestra performed with the Mendelssohn Choir.

OCTOBER 19: Pioneer Club boxing: Max Baer defeated Dutch Weimer.

OCTOBER 21: Canadian Grand Opera performed *Faust*.

OCTOBER 26-31: Bob Morton's Rameses Shrine Circus.

NOVEMBER 5: NHL hockey season opening game; Leafs lost 3-1 to Detroit. The puck was dropped by Hon. H. A. Bruce, Lieutenant-Governor of Ontario, assisted by Jim Norris and G. R. Cottrelle.

NOVEMBER 18: Church meeting, with Rev. Hiram Hull.

1937

JANUARY 6: Crescent Athletic Club professional boxing. The main bout was between Frank Genovese and Sammy Luftspring, won by Luftspring on a technical knockout. Luftspring, who is still involved in the Toronto boxing scene, had refused to represent Canada in the 1936 Olympics because of Hitler's anti-semitic policies.

APRIL 2: Crescent Athletic Club boxing: Canadian Welterweight Championship bout between Sammy Luftspring and Gordon Wallace. Wallace won a split decision.

APRIL 17: International World Hockey Series. England, represented by the Wembley Lions, faced the United States, represented by the Hershey Bears. The Lions won 6-3.

APRIL 18: Memorial Cup junior hockey final. The Winnipeg Monarchs beat the Copper Cliff Redmen 7-0.

APRIL 19: Because the Winnipeg Monarchs had won the Memorial Cup, they were allowed to play against senior opposition in the international series. The Monarchs lost to the Wembley Lions 4-2.

APRIL 23: A tennis tour moved into the building, with Ellsworth Vines and Fred Perry.

APRIL 26: Hockey: Wembley versus Sudbury. Sudbury won the final game of this series that was interrupted by the tennis tournament. From this time on, under building superintendents

Doug Morris and Don MacKenzie, the building has been converted quickly to handle different sports.

APRIL 30: IOF pageant: International Spring Festival.

MAY 1: Toronto May Day labour conference.

MAY 8: Toronto Girl Guides rally.

MAY 19: Opening of the lacrosse season. Marlboros were defeated by Orillia, the Canadian champions, 22-16.

JUNE 1: Crescent Athletic Club boxing: Sammy Luftspring versus George Bland. On this date the government lifted a surcharge on tickets for entertainment events in order to help show business and athletics.

OCTOBER 25-30: Bob Morton's Rameses Shrine Circus.

NOVEMBER 1: Exhibition hockey: Dick Irvin's Blues lost to Eddie Power's Whites 5-3. This began an annual game that was to run for a number of years between players trying out for the Leaf team. It was usually one of the best games of the season.

NOVEMBER 4: NHL opening game for the Leafs. Detroit Red Wings and Toronto tied 2-2. Hon. Gordon Conant, Attorney-General of Ontario, dropped the first puck, assisted by Jim Norris and G. R. Cottrelle.

1938

APRIL 12: Memorial Cup junior hockey final. Oshawa Generals lost 4-0 to the St. Boniface Seals.

APRIL 30: Professional tennis tour: Ellsworth Vines and Fred Perry.

MAY 20-21: Toronto Kennel Club international dog show and greyhound racing exhibition.

SEPTEMBER 18: Jehovah's Witnesses, with Judge Rutherford.

OCTOBER 7: Mann Cup lacrosse final: St. Catharines Athletics defeated the New Westminster Adanacs 18-11.

OCTOBER 8: Paul Whiteman's Orchestra. For $1.50 and $1.00 you had dancing privileges; for 50 cents you had to sit in the green seats and couldn't dance.

OCTOBER 24-29: Bob Morton's Rameses Shrine Circus.

NOVEMBER 3: Opening game of the NHL season for the Leafs. Boston 3, Toronto 2. The puck was dropped by Albert Matthews, Lieutenant-Governor of Ontario, assisted by G. R. Cottrelle and Weston Adams.

NOVEMBER 20: Canadian Jewish Congress public meeting.

NOVEMBER 23: Duke Ellington and his Orchestra.

DECEMBER 5-6: Sonja Henie and Company, with Toronto's Stewart Reburn.

DECEMBER 12: Queensbury Athletic Club boxing: Canadian Welterweight Championship match between Sammy Luftspring and Tommy Bland. Luftspring retained the crown in a split decision.

DECEMBER 23: Christmas Frolic.

1939

FEBRUARY 16: Maple Leaf Athletic Club wrestling: World Heavyweight Championship match between Joe Savoldi and Jim Londos, won by Londos.

FEBRUARY 27: Queensbury Athletic Club boxing: a double card with Sammy Luftspring versus Frankie Genovese and Baby Yack versus Jesse Levals. From the mid-1930s to the mid-1950s there were many more boxing cards at the Gardens than are listed here; only a number of them have been mentioned.

MARCH 6-10: Toronto Skating Club carnival.

MARCH 11: Professional tennis tour: Don Budge, Ellsworth Vines, A. H. Capin, Jr., Dick Skeen.

MARCH 15: Leadership League public meeting.

APRIL 10: Memorial Cup hockey final: Oshawa Generals versus Edmonton Roamers. This was the series in which Billy Taylor starred for Oshawa, and Elmer Kreller of Edmonton was sent out to check him. So persistent was Kreller,

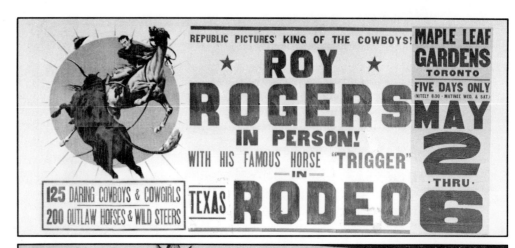

Toronto billboard, 1944.

Public school bond rally.
ALEXANDRA STUDIO

A college basketball tournament, 1946.
ALEXANDRA STUDIO

The big band era at the Gardens.
ALEXANDRA STUDIO

Wartime rally.
ALEXANDRA STUDIO

if not successful, that ever afterward he was called "Elmer the Shadow."

APRIL 20-22: National Electric Show.

APRIL 28: IOF grand pageant: Symbols of Spring.

MAY 2: Tennis: Don Budge versus Fred Perry. For much of the month of September, 1939, very little was taking place at the Gardens, as Canada had declared war on Germany. The President of the Gardens, Conn Smythe, organized his own battalion, the 30th Sportsmens Battery, and he took a lot of good men with him overseas. Soon the Gardens began to serve the war effort with many rallies and bond efforts.

OCTOBER 23-28: Bob Morton's Rameses Shrine Circus.

NOVEMBER 4: Opening NHL game for the Leafs. Boston 5, Toronto 0, the first opening game shut-out in the building.

1940

JANUARY 10: Opening of prep school hockey, with University of Toronto Schools against Upper Canada College. UTS had won the first junior Memorial Cup when it was presented in 1919 in honour the Canadian war dead, but in 1940 lost 10-1 to UCC.

FEBRUARY 21: Senior city hockey championship game in aid of the Finnish Fund. Goodyear beat the University of Toronto 4-0.

MARCH 4: Maple Leaf Athletic Club boxing: World Championship bout between George Pace and Lou Salica. They battled to a draw after fifteen rounds.

MARCH 18: Conservative leader Hon. R. J. Manion addressed an Ontario Conservative Party public meeting.

APRIL 20: Allan Cup hockey playoffs: Kirkland Lake Blue Devils defeated Calgary Stampeders 8-5 in the first game. Two of the players on the Kirkland Lake team, Mike Kowchinak and Johnny McCreedy, usually ended up in different mining towns each year, and that town would win the Allan Cup. McCreedy, who later played

with the Toronto Maple Leafs, became president of INCO.

OCTOBER 7: First game for the Mann Cup, symbol of the senior lacrosse championship of Canada. Vancouver beat St. Catharines 14-9.

OCTOBER 18: Toronto Star Coliseum Chorus with the Toronto Symphony Orchestra.

OCTOBER 21-26: Bob Morton's Rameses Shrine Circus.

NOVEMBER 2: Opening game of the season for Toronto. New York Rangers defeated the Leafs 4-1. Although many of the hockey players in the NHL were going off to war, it was decided to continue with the league and the many attractions at the Gardens in an attempt to aid the overseas effort.

NOVEMBER 8: Sports Service League bingo night. During the war there were many such nights at the Gardens, only a very few of which are listed here. This was another way to raise money for war causes and to provide a different kind of entertainment.

NOVEMBER 21: Queensbury Athletic Club wrestling: The Golden Terror versus Ivan Rasputin. Ladies and soldiers in uniform were charged an admission price of 25 cents.

DECEMBER 6: Canadian Seaman's Union public meeting. Chief speaker was Doris Neilson, M.P. for North Battleford.

1941

JANUARY 10: Queensbury Athletic Club wrestling: Wild Bill Longson defeated Frank Taylor and Whipper Billy Watson beat Jack Russell. This was the first major Whipper Watson fight. Watson became a famous wrestler during the war years and after.

FEBRUARY 13: Toronto War Savings Committee youth rally.

MARCH 24: Canadian War Service Fund meeting, with Wendell Wilkie.

APRIL 21: First game of the Memorial Cup hockey finals, in which the Montreal Royals lost to the Winnipeg Rangers 4-2, with Winnipeg the eventual winners of the series.

APRIL 25: Professional tennis: Alice Marble, Mary Hardwick, Don Budge and Bill Tilden. Marble and Hardwick were the first woman athletes to appear at the Gardens.

MAY 10: 48th Highlanders bazaar.

MAY 21: Toronto Board of Education meeting, with a demonstration of physical culture and cadet training.

MAY 27-31: Water Follies, with stars of the World's Fair Aquacade, including Buster Crabbe.

JUNE 3: Women's Victory Loan rally. Dorothy Thompson was the speaker.

JULY 8: Public meeting under the auspices of the *Canadian Tribune*. The chief speaker was Vladimir Steffanson.

JULY 29: Canadian Corps Association public meeting.

OCTOBER 17-18: Toronto Star Coliseum Chorus with the Toronto Symphony Orchestra.

OCTOBER 20-25: Bob Morton's Rameses Shrine Circus.

OCTOBER 26: Public meeting organized by the *Canadian Tribune*. The speakers were Doris Neilson, M.P., Leslie Roberts and A. A. MacLeod.

OCTOBER 27: Cab Calloway and his Cotton Club Orchestra. Before 6 p.m. the admission was $1.00; after 6 it was $1.25.

NOVEMBER 1: Opening Leaf hockey game. Rangers 4, Leafs 3. The United States Consul General dropped the first puck.

NOVEMBER 18-21: Ice Follies. This was the first visit of the Follies, a show that has been to the Gardens every year since.

NOVEMBER 24: Toronto Boxing Club: Canadian Welterweight Championship between Dave Castilloux and Sonny Jones. Castilloux won a unanimous ten-round decision.

NOVEMBER 29: Brooklyn Americans defeated 8-2 by the Toronto Maple Leafs. This was the first visit of the Brooklyn team to the Gardens.

DECEMBER 20: Canada Starch Company Christmas Frolic with Red Foster. Foster was later to become a great crusader for the

mentally retarded and staged some of his Olympics for the Mentally Retarded at the Gardens.

1942

JANUARY 30: Moose Ecclestone Night. The hockey community often bands together to help those of their numbers who have come on unfortunate times. Moose Ecclestone did a lot for minor hockey in Toronto before his tragic death. St. Catharines juniors played a game against the Marlies, and in an unprecedented move the NHL All Stars played a game against the Toronto Maple Leafs, with proceeds to charity.

FEBRUARY 12: Queensbury Athletic Club wrestling: Earl McCready defeated Nanjo Singh for the British Empire Title.

FEBRUARY 18: Victory Loan public meeting, with Gracie Fields.

FEBRUARY 23: Military hockey tournament: Woodstock, Kingston, Borden, Royal Military College, Petawawa, Hamilton. Camp Borden beat Hamilton 15-3 for the title.

MARCH 2: Victory Loan meeting. The chief speaker was Mrs. Borden Harriman.

MARCH 7: Military hockey championship: Camp Borden was defeated 11-2 by RCAF Ottawa. Milt Schmidt of Ottawa had three goals and two assists.

APRIL 18: Lots of hockey at the Gardens. At 3 p.m. RCAF Ottawa played Port Arthur Bearcats in the Allan Cup playoffs. Then, at 8 p.m. the Toronto Maple Leafs played the Detroit Red Wings for the Stanley Cup. This was the seventh game, and the Leafs beat Detroit 3-0. It has been the only time in hockey history that an NHL club lost the first three games of the finals, then went on to win four straight. Over 16,000 fans attended the game, to that time the largest crowd to watch a hockey game in Canada.

APRIL 25: Allan Cup finals: Ottawa RCAF defeated Port Arthur 7-1.

MAY 9: Roller Skating Follies, the first roller skating in the building. The Roller Derby would come later.

MAY 16: Imperial Order, Daughters of the Empire (IODE), 48th Highlanders Chapter.

MAY 26-30: Water Follies, with Buster Crabbe.

JUNE 13: Dancing to the Modernaires.

JUNE 20: Dancing to Ned Hamill.

JUNE 21: Al St. John's Orchestra, sponsored by Jean Pengelly and the Guardsmen.

JUNE 22-25: Rotary Club convention. In attendance was the Governor-General of Canada, The Earl of Athlone, and appearing were the Toronto Symphony Orchestra, Mona Bates and Gracie Fields. This was the first of many Rotary Club visits to the Gardens, and the Rotarians also began to sponsor many cultural events in the building, at the encouragement of Stanley Reid.

JUNE 29: Salute to Canada's Army, with Paul Robeson, the great American baritone.

JULY 2: Dance and vaudeville show.

JULY 17: Civil Liberties Union.

JULY 21: Lions Club.

SEPTEMBER 21: Public war rally.

OCTOBER 7: Mann Cup lacrosse finals: Mimico-Brampton Combines defeated New Westminster Salmonbellies 10-7.

OCTOBER 13: Public meeting of the Citizen's Committee, with Tim Buck, Hon. Leopold Macaulay, Hon. Mitchell Hepburn.

OCTOBER 19-24: Bob Morton's Rameses Shrine Circus.

OCTOBER 26-28: One of the biggest Victory Loan pageants, with the Dionne quintuplets.

OCTOBER 29: Annual pre-season game for the Leafs, sponsored by the Kiwanis Club and the Victory Loan Committee. Syl Apps' Blues defeated Nick Metz's Whites 3-2, with proceeds of $10,000 to charity.

OCTOBER 31: NHL opener for the Leafs. This was the first time that the season opened in October. Leafs beat the New York Rangers 7-2. The opening face-off ceremony was performed by Private Alex Chisholm, who was decorated for his service at the battle of Dieppe.

NOVEMBER 17-20: Ice Follies.

NOVEMBER 25: Aid to Russia public meeting, with Wendell Wilkie.

1943

FEBRUARY 5: Senior OHA hockey: an Aid to Russia benefit between the RCAF and the Marlboro service teams.

MARCH 6: Canadian Red Cross youth rally.

MARCH 8-12: Ice Capades of 1943. This was the first time that the Ice Capades, a show put together to compete with the Ice Follies, appeared at the Gardens.

MAY 3: Victory Loan rally.

MAY 6-8: Roller Follies of 1943.

MAY 10: Victory Loan rally, CWAC graduation and tattoo, National War Finance Committee meeting.

MAY 11-12: Sigmund Romberg and his Orchestra.

MAY 15: 48th Highlanders carnival night.

JUNE 22: A Salute to Our Russian Ally, under the auspices of the Council for Canadian-Soviet Friendship.

SEPTEMBER 8: Canadian Jewish Congress.

SEPTEMBER 12: Fitch Band Wagon, with Guy Lombardo and his Royal Canadians. Admission was only through the purchase of war savings stamps.

OCTOBER 18-23: Shriners Charity Circus.

OCTOBER 30: Opening NHL hockey game for the Leafs. Toronto beat the New York Rangers 5-2. Assisted by Ed Bickle, George Drew, Premier of Ontario, officiated at the opening face-off.

NOVEMBER 14: War veterans memorial service and a thanksgiving service for Soviet victories, organized by the National Council for Canadian-Soviet Friendship.

NOVEMBER 26: Kinsmen bingo, proceeds to the Milk for Britain Fund. There were many such nights during the war.

DECEMBER 6-10: Ice Capades. This was the second visit of the Ice Capades within a year, the only time that this has happened.

DECEMBER 31: New Year's Eve dance, with the orchestras of Ken Good and Don Romanelli.

1944

JANUARY 8: Leaf Babe Pratt contributed six assists, a club record for a defenceman. Toronto 12, Boston 3.

FEBRUARY 18: Food Industry war savings stamp drive, with Quentin Reynolds.

APRIL 15: Memorial Cup hockey final: Oshawa Generals defeated the Trail Smoke Eaters 9-2.

MAY 2-6: Texas Rodeo, with Roy Rogers and Trigger. This was the first rodeo in the building.

MAY 9: Victory Loan rally, under the auspices of the National War Finance Committee, starring Gracie Fields.

JUNE 3: 48th Highlanders bazaar.

JUNE 23: Public meeting organized by the National Council for Canadian-Soviet Friendship.

JUNE 26-JULY 1: Garden Bros. Circus, sponsored by the Kiwanis Club.

SEPTEMBER 20: Bob Hope Show. Seats were sold for war savings stamps.

SEPTEMBER 25-26: Phil Spitalny and his "Hour of Charm," including his All-Girl Orchestra.

OCTOBER 1: People's Church meeting.

OCTOBER 7: Mann Cup lacrosse final: New Westminster Salmonbellies defeated 17-10 by the St. Catharines Athletics in the first game of a best of three final.

OCTOBER 8: People's Church meeting.

OCTOBER 10: Lacrosse for the Camp Borden championship. Camp Borden Combines defeated No. 2 Armored Corps 12-6.

OCTOBER 28: Leafs' NHL opener. Toronto 2, New York Rangers 1. J. G. Parker, War Financial Chairman, dropped the first puck. With him was J. P. Bickell.

OCTOBER 30: The Andrews Sisters.

NOVEMBER 12: Jehovah's Witness Service.

NOVEMBER 19: Navy League of Canada.

NOVEMBER 27-DECEMBER 1: Ice Capades.

DECEMBER 19: Tommy Dorsey and his Orchestra.

1945

FEBRUARY 5-9: Ice Follies of 1945.

FEBRUARY 16: Toronto Police Association concert. This was to become an annual event.

APRIL 14: Memorial Cup hockey final: St. Michael's College defeated Moose Jaw Canucks 8-5 in the opening game.

APRIL 22: Leafs beat Detroit 2-1 for the Stanley Cup, with the seventh and deciding game in Detroit.

APRIL 30: Jack Allen's boxing show.

MAY 1: Gene Krupa and his Orchestra and dance.

MAY 7-12: Texas Rodeo with Roy Rogers and Trigger.

MAY 23: Tommy Dorsey's Orchestra and dance.

JUNE 10: United Church of Canada's twentieth anniversary meeting.

JUNE 15: Charlie Spivak's Orchestra and dance.

JUNE 16: Toronto churches youth rally.

JUNE 23: Woody Herman and his Orchestra and dance.

JUNE 23: Ukrainian Festival.

SEPTEMBER 11-15: Roller Skating Vanities.

OCTOBER 3: Allied aircraft reconversion meeting.

OCTOBER 5: Tony Pastor and his Orchestra.

OCTOBER 15-30: Bob Morton's Rameses Shrine Circus.

OCTOBER 22: Phil Spitalny and his All-Girl Orchestra.

OCTOBER 27: Opening Leaf game, with Leafs and Bruins tying 1-1. The opening ceremony was attended by Ed Bickle and six Victoria Cross holders: Cpl. Fred Topham, Pvt. Smoky

Smith, Major Fred Tilson, Lt. Col. Paul Triquet, Lt. Col. D. V. Currie and Major J. J. Mahony. Pvt. Smith dropped the puck.

OCTOBER 30: Victory Loan rally, with Fibber McGee and Molly.

NOVEMBER 9: Girls softball: Jax of New Orleans, the tournament winners, played Sunday Morning Class and Simpson's Senior Ladies.

NOVEMBER 21: National Council for Canadian-Soviet Friendship meeting, with the Dean of Canterbury, "The Red Dean."

NOVEMBER 26-30: Ice Capades.

DECEMBER 31: Ellis McLintock and his Orchestra.

1946

A power plant was installed at the Gardens during 1946.

JANUARY 16: Basketball, sponsored by the Rotary Club. There were games between the University of Toronto and the University of Western Ontario, and a professional game between the Fort Wayne Zollners and the Rochester Royals. This was the first basketball at the Gardens.

JANUARY 29: Gyro Remembrance Night, with the Toronto Symphony.

FEBRUARY 4-8: Ice Follies of 1946.

FEBRUARY 22: Rotary Club basketball: Assumption College of Windsor versus Tip Tops; Dow Athletic Club versus Hayes Hellcats.

MARCH 31: Reception for Cardinal McGuigan, the first Canadian Roman Catholic Cardinal.

APRIL 13: Memorial Cup hockey final: Winnipeg Monarchs defeated St. Michael's College 3-2 in this opening game.

APRIL 25: Simpson's Teen-Town Time Dance.

APRIL 28: Canadian Council of Churches Service of Witness.

MAY 1: Professional tennis: Bobby Riggs and Don Budge.

MAY 3: Eleventh Annual Drummer's Ball.

MAY 7: Board of Education physical training demonstration.

MAY 13-18: S.Q. Ranch Rodeo with Gene Autry.

JUNE 14: Council for Canadian-Soviet Friendship meeting.

JUNE 15: Toronto Youth for Christ rally.

JUNE 26: Canadian Legion rally.

AUGUST 24: Ukrainian concert.

SEPTEMBER 10-14: Roller Skating Vanities of 1946.

SEPTEMBER 30: Dominion Lacrosse Championship: St. Catharines Athletics defeated New Westminster Salmonbellies 11-10.

OCTOBER 9-14: Bob Morton's Rameses Shrine Circus.

OCTOBER 19: Leafs' NHL opener: Toronto 6, Detroit 3. Mayor Robert Saunders of Toronto dropped the first puck.

OCTOBER 30: Hadassah Bazaar.

NOVEMBER 1: The first professional indoor basketball game in the National Basketball Association was played at the Gardens. New York Knickerbockers defeated Toronto Huskies 68-66.

NOVEMBER 5: Fritz Kreisler concert.

NOVEMBER 13: Youth for Christ rally.

DECEMBER 2-6: Ice Capades.

1947

Herculite glass was installed around the boards of the hockey rink during 1947, the first in the world. Electronic clocks were installed to time players individually.

JANUARY 8: Howie Meeker scored five goals in one game, a club record until 1975. This was also a record for most goals in one game by a rookie.

FEBRUARY 3-7: Ice Follies of 1947.

FEBRUARY 24: The Alex Templeton Show.

MARCH 19: Top price for tickets to a Leaf game became $3.00.

MARCH 23: Ken Soble's Amateur Show for the Ontario Society for Crippled Children.

APRIL 19: Leafs beat Montreal 2-1 to win the Stanley Cup.

APRIL 26: Allan Cup hockey final: Winnipeg Royals versus Calgary Stampeders.

APRIL 29-30: Ice Revue, starring Barbara Ann Scott.

MAY 2: Kiwanis Club: Orpheus Male Chorus.

MAY 9: Drummer's Ball.

MAY 15: Wrestling: Lou Thesz and Whipper Billy Watson fought to a draw which allowed Thesz to keep the World Title.

JUNE 23: Frank Tunney's pro boxing. Lil' Arthur King versus Spider Armstrong. King was the decisive winner.

AUGUST 18-19: Roman Choir.

SEPTEMBER 18: Queensbury Athletic Club wrestling: Whipper Billy Watson versus Primo Carnera, with Watson the winner.

SEPTEMBER 23-27: Roller Skating Vanities of 1947.

OCTOBER 6-11: Rameses Shrine Circus.

OCTOBER 13: NHL All Star Game: The Stanley Cup champion Leafs were defeated by the NHL All Stars, 4-3.

OCTOBER 18: Opening of the NHL season for the Leafs. Toronto 2, Detroit 2. Field Marshal Lord Alexander, Governor-General of Canada, officiated at the face-off.

OCTOBER 19: Ken Soble's Amateur Show.

OCTOBER 20: Simpson's Teen-Town Time Dance.

OCTOBER 28: Hadassah Bazaar.

NOVEMBER 17-20: Ice Capades.

1948

A new marquee was built during 1948. Conn Smythe was back from the war, and he became president of Maple Leaf Gardens. His presidency was to last until 1961, when the threesome of Harold Ballard, Stafford Smythe and John Bassett took over.

JANUARY 5: Frank Tunney pro boxing: Phil Terranova versus Lil' Arthur King.

JANUARY 21: Police concert with the Detroit Symphony Orchestra.

FEBRUARY 2-6: Ice Follies of 1948.

FEBRUARY 19: Queensbury Athletic Club wrestling: Lou Thesz versus Whipper Billy Watson. Ladies now were charged $1.00, half the price of admission for men. Watson went down to defeat.

MARCH 21: Ken Soble's Amateur Show for the Ontario Society for Crippled Children. Over the years the Gardens has given and contributed in various ways millions of dollars to this society.

MARCH 24: The Toronto Maple Leafs played the Boston Bruins in the Stanley Cup playoffs. A service charge of 25 cents was added to tickets for the NHL pension fund. Toronto eventually played the Detroit Red Wings in the final and swept the series in four straight games.

APRIL 10: Detroit 2 and Toronto 4, the second game of the Stanley Cup final.

APRIL 24: Memorial Cup hockey finals: Port Arthur Bruins versus the Barrie Flyers.

MAY 10-11: Olympic basketball tryouts: Western Mustangs versus the British Columbia Thunderbirds; Montreal YMHA versus the Vancouver Cloverleafs.

MAY 14-15: Phil Spitalny's All-Girl Orchestra.

MAY 16: Zionist meeting.

JUNE 15-19: Aqua Parade of 1948.

OCTOBER 4-9: Bob Morton's Rameses Shrine Circus.

OCTOBER 11: Mann Cup lacrosse final: Hamilton Tigers versus New Westminster Adanacs. New Westminster won.

OCTOBER 16: Opening game of the NHL hockey season for the Leafs. From this time on the season opening was to settle around mid-October. Boston beat the Leafs 4-1. Brigadier General H. D. Crerer dropped the first puck.

OCTOBER 22: Simpson's Teen-Town Time Dance, with proceeds to the Community Chest.

NOVEMBER 2: Hadassah Bazaar.

NOVEMBER 8-12: Ice Capades.

1949

JANUARY 31-FEBRUARY 4: Ice Follies of 1949.

FEBRUARY 16: Toronto Police Association concert.

MARCH 3: Queensbury Athletic Club wrestling. Fred Atkins versus Whipper Billy Watson. Fred Atkins, who snatched the World Title from Watson, was later to return to the Gardens as a physical training instructor for the Leafs.

APRIL 3: Ken Soble's Amateur Show for the Ontario Society for Crippled Children.

APRIL 16: The Leafs beat the Detroit Red Wings 3-1 to win the Stanley Cup for the third straight year.

MAY 4: Allan Cup hockey final. Regina Caps versus the Ottawa Senators. The Senators took the Cup.

MAY 10-14: Ice Revue of 1949.

MAY 15: Massed bands in connection with military week.

JUNE 21: Liberal Party rally, with The Right Hon. Louis St. Laurent, Prime Minister, as the speaker.

JUNE 24-26: Watch Tower Bible and Tract Society.

AUGUST 8-11: Order of the Eastern Star.

AUGUST 18-19: Miss Canada Beauty Pageant.

SEPTEMBER 19: Frank Tunney's pro boxing: Canadian heavyweight boxing tournament.

OCTOBER 3-8: Bob Morton's Rameses Shrine Circus.

OCTOBER 10: NHL All Star Game: The All Stars versus the Toronto Maple Leafs. The Leafs won.

OCTOBER 12: The Bob Hope Show, with Jerry Colonna and Les Brown.

OCTOBER 15: Opening of the NHL hockey season for the Leafs: Toronto 4, Chicago Black Hawks 4.

NOVEMBER 7-11: Ice Capades.

1950

JANUARY 23: Frank Tunney's pro boxing: Spider Thompson versus Alan McFater, with McFater the winner.

JANUARY 30-FEBRUARY 3: Ice Follies of 1950.

FEBRUARY 21: Toronto Police concert.

MARCH 20: Frank Tunney's pro boxing: Alan McFater versus Buddy Hayes. McFater won.

MARCH 27: Order of the Eastern Star Fun Parade.

APRIL 2: Radio Show of Stars for the Ontario Society for Crippled Children.

APRIL 29: Memorial Cup finals for the junior hockey supremacy of Canada. The Montreal Junior Canadiens beat the Regina Pats. Both teams were the property of the Montreal Canadiens.

MAY 7: Canadian Slav Committee public concert.

MAY 15: Spike Jones Show.

MAY 23: Shrine meeting.

MAY 26: Manitoba Flood Relief Fund. The Province of Manitoba suffered a disaster when the Red River overflowed and flooded hundreds of thousands of acres.

MAY 31: The Jack Benny Show.

JUNE 11: United Church meeting.

AUGUST 14: Canadian Council of Churches youth rally.

OCTOBER 1-7: Bob Morton's Rameses Shrine Circus.

OCTOBER 8: Mann Cup lacrosse final: New Westminster versus Owen Sound. New Westminster won.

OCTOBER 14: Opening game of the NHL hockey season. Chicago Blacks Hawks beat the Leafs 2-1. The first puck was dropped by Brigadier General John Rockingham.

Nicolai Fadeyechev and Marina Kondratieva in Giselle.

Princess Elizabeth.
ALEXANDRA STUDIO

Lester Pearson.
ALEXANDRA STUDIO

Carmen, *1959.*

Steer-riding at the Gardens.

NOVEMBER 7: Horace Heidt and his Orchestra, sponsored by the Rotary Club.

NOVEMBER 13-17: Ice Capades.

1951

JANUARY 29-FEBRUARY 2: Ice Follies of 1951.

FEBRUARY 8: Queensbury Athletic Club wrestling: Lord Athol Layton's first featured bout at the Gardens, this night against Fred Atkins. Lord Layton won by decision.

FEBRUARY 12: Toronto newsboys' boxing show.

MARCH 18: Radio Show of Stars for the Ontario Society for Crippled Children.

APRIL 21: Toronto Maple Leafs beat the Montreal Canadiens 3-2 in the fifth game of the finals to win the Stanley Cup. This was the only Cup the Leafs won in the 1950s. The defence-man who scored the winning goal, Bill Barilko, was killed during the summer in a northern Ontario airplane accident.

APRIL 23: Frank Tunney's pro boxing: Solly Cantor versus "Sunny" Dave Shade. Cantor was awarded a draw in the ninth round.

MAY 8: Alexander Cup of hockey. Field Marshal Lord Alexander, the Governor-General of Canada, had donated a trophy, and it was competed for by the Valleyfield Braves and the St. Michael's Monarchs. The Valleyfield team won.

MAY 20: Watch Tower Bible and Tract Society.

JUNE 30: Ukrainian Canadian Jubilee Festival.

OCTOBER 1-6: Rameses Shrine Circus.

OCTOBER 9: NHL All Star game. The first team All Stars played the second team All Stars, a new format.

OCTOBER 10: Biggest Show of '51.

OCTOBER 13: At 1:50 p.m. there was an exhibition game between Weston Dukes and the St. Mike's Junior B team. At 3 p.m. the Chicago Black Hawks played an abbreviated game with the Leafs solely for the benefit of royal visitors, Her Royal Highness, Princess Elizabeth, and His Royal Highness, Prince Philip. At 8:30 the two pro teams took to the ice again for the season opener, and Chicago beat the Leafs 3-1. Princess Elizabeth dropped the opening puck for the 3 p.m. game.

OCTOBER 23: Basketball: The Harlem Globetrotters played the Toledo Mercurys, and the Minneapolis Lakers played the Philadelphia Warriors. This was the first visit of the Globetrotters to the Gardens, and they have been coming yearly every since.

OCTOBER 29: Roy Ward Dickson Show.

NOVEMBER 12-16: Ice Capades.

1952

Televised hockey games begin in 1952.

JANUARY 28-FEBRUARY 1: Ice Follies of 1952.

FEBRUARY 6: The death of King George VI resulted in the cancellation of the second Leafs game in the team's history.

FEBRUARY 15: Memorial service for His Majesty, King George VI.

MARCH 3: Fun Parade, with The Roy Ward Dickson Show.

APRIL 6: All Star Radio Show for the Ontario Society for Crippled Children.

APRIL 22: Memorial Cup hockey playoffs: Guelph Biltmores versus the Regina Pats. The Biltmores won.

APRIL 23-29: Hollywood Ice Revue, starring Barbara Ann Scott.

MAY 6-8: White Shrine annual convention.

MAY 11: Canadian Peace Congress meeting.

MAY 26-29: The first visit of the Metropolitan Opera. The Gardens was ingeniously transformed from an arena into an opera house. *Aida, La Bohème, Carmen* and *Rigoletto* were performed.

JUNE 1: Incorporated Synod of the Diocese of Toronto.

JUNE 6: The Cisco Kid and the Western Roundup.

AUGUST 7: Queensbury Athletic Club wrestling: Canadian Open Team Championship.

SEPTEMBER 20: Biggest Show of '52.

SEPTEMBER 29-OCTOBER 4: Bob Morton's Rameses Shrine Circus.

OCTOBER 5: Mann Cup lacrosse finals: Vancouver versus Peterborough. Vancouver won.

OCTOBER 11: Opening game of the Leafs' NHL hockey season: Chicago beat the Leafs 6-2. The face-off ceremony was performed by Conn Smythe.

OCTOBER 14: Boxing: The White Hope Tournament.

OCTOBER 27: Super Fun Parade with The Roy Ward Dickson Show.

OCTOBER 28: Dean Martin and Jerry Lewis Show. Top price was $4.00.

NOVEMBER 10-14: Ice Capades.

1953

JANUARY 8: Queensbury Athletic Club wrestling: Chief Big Heart versus Gorgeous George. Gorgeous George won.

JANUARY 27: Professional tennis: Frank Sedgman and Ken McGregor versus Jack Kramer and Pancho Segura.

FEBRUARY 2-6: Ice Follies of 1953.

FEBRUARY 13: The Gene Autry Show.

MARCH 2: Fun Parade with Roy Ward Dickson.

MARCH 29: All-Star Radio Show for the Ontario Society for Crippled Children.

APRIL 6: Little NHL hockey tournament: Winnipeg Canadiens versus Midland Bruins.

APRIL 12: Oldtimers hockey tournament.

APRIL 13: Horace Heidt Show.

APRIL 15: Professional tennis: Jack Kramer, Pancho Segura, Frank Sedgman, Rod McGregor.

MAY 25-30: The Metropolitan Opera Company, performing *La Forza Del Destino, Carmen, Tosca,*

Lohengrin, Rigoletto, Samson and Delilah. Prices were $10.00 tops, the highest at the Gardens to that time.

AUGUST 7: Liberal Party rally. The chief speaker was The Right Hon. Louis St. Laurent, Prime Minister of Canada.

AUGUST 21-22: Federated Women's Institutes of Canada pageant.

SEPTEMBER 18: Guard Republican Band of Paris.

SEPTEMBER 26: Biggest Show of 1953.

SEPTEMBER 26-OCTOBER 3: Bob Morton's Rameses Shrine Circus.

OCTOBER 10: Opening hockey game of the seasons for the Leafs. Toronto defeated Chicago 6-2. The Bickell Cup was presented for the first time; Ted Kennedy was the recipient. Neilly Palmer, a business associate of Bickell, and Mrs. J. B. Paulin, Bickell's sister, dropped the first puck.

OCTOBER 27-29: Sadler's Wells, the first major ballet to play at the Gardens. *Sleeping Beauty* and *Swan Lake* were performed, with a top price for tickets of $6.00. This was the first major company to appear in Canada, and it pointed out the need for large Canadian theatres to stage ballet. Within a few years, fine theatres were built in Toronto, Montreal, Vancouver, Edmonton and Calgary. This appearance also gave the impetus for Celia Franca to found the National Ballet Company.

NOVEMBER 16-20: Ice Capades.

1954

JANUARY 20: Professional tennis: Frank Sedgman, Donald Budge, José Gonzales and Pancho Segura.

JANUARY 25: Youth for Christ religious meeting.

FEBRUARY 1-5: Ice Follies of 1954.

MARCH 1: Fun Parade with Roy Ward Dickson.

APRIL 11: All Star Radio Show for the Ontario Society for Crippled Children.

APRIL 27-MAY 1: Hollywood Ice Revue.

MAY 8: Liberace and Company. Top price was $4.80.

MAY 9: Memorial Cup hockey finals: St. Catharines versus Edmonton. St. Catharines won.

MAY 24-29: Metropolitan Opera Company, performing *Lucia di Lammermoor, Aida, Barber of Seville, La Traviata, Faust, Rigoletto.*

JUNE 14: Spike Jones.

JULY 22: Queensbury Athletic Club wrestling: Whipper Billy Watson versus Killer Kowalski. Watson won by decision.

SEPTEMBER 27-OCTOBER 2: Bob Morton's Rameses Shrine Circus.

OCTOBER 5: Mantovani.

OCTOBER 9: Opening game of the Leafs hockey season. Toronto 3, Chicago 3. Marilyn Bell and Gus Ryder were present for the opening face-off.

OCTOBER 18-20: London's Festival Ballet. Performed were *Esmerelda, Swan Lake, Scheherazade, Alice in Wonderland, Napoli, Vision of Marguerite,* and *The Nutcracker.*

NOVEMBER 22-26: Ice Capades.

DECEMBER 14-16: Old Vic Company produced *A Midsummer Night's Dream.* Shakespeare at the Gardens cost $6.00 tops.

1955

Escalators installed at the Gardens during 1955, the first in any arena in North America.

JANUARY 31-FEBRUARY 4: Ice Follies of 1955.

APRIL 3: Timmy's Easter Parade of Stars. This was the first time a Timmy was used as a symbol for Easter Seals and the Crippled Children's campaign.

MAY 11: George Formby Variety Show.

MAY 23-28: Metropolitan Opera Company. Performed were Puccini's *Madame Butterfly,* Mascagni's *Cavalleria Rusticana,* Leoncavallo's *Pagliacci,* Verdi's *La Traviata,* Puccini's *Tosca,* Giordano's *Andrea Chenier,* and Bizet's *Carmen.*

AUGUST 16-21: World Convention of Churches of Christ.

SEPTEMBER 19: Mantovani.

SEPTEMBER 26-OCTOBER 1: Bob Morton's Rameses Shrine Circus.

OCTOBER 2: Youth for Christ rally, with Billy Graham.

OCTOBER 8: Leafs NHL hockey opener. Toronto beat Detroit 4-2. Ted Kennedy, who was retiring from the Leafs, and Col. W. A. H. MacBrien were present at the opening ceremony.

OCTOBER 11: Scots Guard Band, presented by the Variety Club. This was one of the first bands to come over from Britain.

OCTOBER 27: Queensbury Athletic Club wrestling: Yukon Eric defeated Doug Hepburn.

NOVEMBER 21-25: Ice Capades.

DECEMBER 13-15: Sadler's Wells Ballet.

1956

Lounge built on east side of Gardens during 1956.

JANUARY 30-FEBRUARY 3: Ice Follies of 1956. This show is now known as Shipstads and Johnson Ice Follies.

MARCH 25: Timmy's Easter Parade of Stars for the Ontario Society for Crippled Children.

APRIL 23: Jack Dempsey's heavyweight tournament.

APRIL 27: Memorial Cup finals: Toronto Marlboros versus the Regina Pats. The Marlboros won.

APRIL 30: Bill Haley and his Comets were the first to bring rock and roll into the Gardens. It was to be an important sound in the building from here on in.

MAY 28-JUNE 2: The Metropolitan Opera, with Verdi's *Aida,* Gounod's *Faust,* Bizet's *Carmen,* Strauss' *Die Fledermaus,* Puccini's *La Bohème* and Verdi's *Rigoletto.*

JUNE 11: Queensbury Athletic Club boxing: George Chuvalo versus Johnny Arthur. Chuvalo won.

JULY 16: Rock and Roll Show: top record stars of 1956.

SEPTEMBER 16: Mann Cup lacrosse final: Nanaimo Timbermen versus Peterborough Trailermen. The Timbermen won.

SEPTEMBER 23: Incorporated Synod of the Diocese of Toronto meeting.

SEPTEMBER 29: Rock and Roll Show: The Biggest in Person Show of 1956.

OCTOBER 1-6: Rameses Shrine Circus.

OCTOBER 13: NHL hockey opener. Detroit 4, Toronto 1. This was the twenty-fifth anniversary of the team, and the opening ceremony featured members of the first Leaf Stanley Cup team.

OCTOBER 15-16: Royal Danish Ballet.

OCTOBER 22: Queensbury Athletic Club boxing: George Chuvalo versus Howard King. Chuvalo won.

NOVEMBER 26-30: Ice Capades.

DECEMBER 12: Greater Evangelistic Crusade of Toronto. Chief speaker was Billy Graham.

1957

Lounge built on west side of Gardens during 1957.

JANUARY 28-FEBRUARY 1: Shipstads and Johnson Ice Follies of 1957.

FEBRUARY 18: Rock and Roll Show.

MARCH 16: Toronto Maple Leafs set a club record with most goals in one game: Leafs 14, New York Rangers 1.

MARCH 25: Queensbury Athletic Club boxing: Lil' Arthur King versus Ralph "Tiger" Jones; George Chuvalo versus Moses Graham. Jones and Chuvalo won.

APRIL 2: Elvis Presley. Admittance was $3.50 for the best seats, and there were shows at 6 p.m. and 9 p.m.

APRIL 14: Perry Como appeared in Timmy's Easter Parade of Stars for the Easter Seal Campaign.

APRIL 23: Allan Cup hockey: The Whitby Dunlops versus the Spokane Flyers. After winning the Canadian title, the Dunlops, from the small Ontario town of Whitby, Ontario, went on to win the world hockey title in Oslo, Norway, in 1958. Wren Blair was manager and Sid Smith, an ex-Leaf captain, was coach.

APRIL 29: Rock and Roll Show: Biggest Show of Stars for 1957.

MAY 25: Pat Boone.

MAY 27-JUNE 1: Metropolitan Opera Company, *The Marriage of Figaro*, *La Traviata*, *Il Trovatoro*, *Carmen*, *Tosca* and *La Bohème* were performed.

JUNE 4: Liberal rally. Chief speaker was The Right Hon. Louis St. Laurent, Prime Minister of Canada.

SEPTEMBER 14: Rock and Roll: Biggest Show of Stars for 1957.

SEPTEMBER 26: Black Watch Regimental Band, with the Massed Pipes and Highland Dancers.

SEPTEMBER 30-OCTOBER 5: Rameses Shrine Circus.

OCTOBER 12: Leafs NHL opener. Seats were now $4.00 tops. Detroit beat Toronto 5-3. John S. Kilgour, Chairman of the Toronto United Appeal Chairman, officiated at the opening face-off.

NOVEMBER 22: International hockey: Whitby Dunlops versus Moscow Dynamo. This was the first time a Russian hockey team had played in the Gardens, and Whitby beat them 7-2. The Russians, although they have dominated world hockey since 1961, have never beaten a Canadian team in the building.

NOVEMBER 25-30: Ice Capades.

1958

New press box was built on the south side of the Gardens during 1958, and the organ was installed.

JANUARY 13-15: The Royal Ballet (formerly Sadler's Wells). It was a wonderful way to begin the year. Nineteen fifty-eight and 1959 were to be the two biggest cultural years in Gardens' history. Margot Fonteyn performed in *Sleeping Beauty*, Rowena Jackson in *Swan Lake, Les Patineurs, Petrouchka,* and *Birthday Offering*.

JANUARY 20: Rock and Roll Show: America's greatest teen-age recording stars.

FEBRUARY 3-7: Shipstads and Johnson Ice Follies of 1958.

MARCH 30: Timmy's Easter Parade of Stars for the Easter Seal Campaign.

APRIL 21: Rock and Roll Show.

MAY 6: World Tennis Inc.: Lew Hoad, Pancho Gonzales, Tony Trabert, Pancho Segura, Jack Kramer, Ken Rosewall.

MAY 9-10: Moiseyev Ballet, later the Moiseyev Dance Company. Top admission price was $6.00.

MAY 26-31: Metropolitan Opera Company: *Eugene Onegin, Madame Butterfly, Barber of Seville, Samson and Delilah, Aida* and *Faust*.

JUNE 29: Baptist Youth World Conference. Prime Minister John Diefenbaker was the guest speaker.

SEPTEMBER 15: Queensbury Athletic Club boxing: George Chuvalo versus James J. Parker, with Chuvalo the winner.

SEPTEMBER 24: Grenadier Guards and the Massed Pipes and Highland Dancers of the Scots Guards.

SEPTEMBER 29-OCTOBER 4: Rameses Shrine Circus.

OCTOBER 11: NHL hockey opener. Chicago beat Toronto 3-1. Retired Leaf star Clarence "Hap" Day dropped the first puck.

OCTOBER 21: Sol Hurok presented Maria Callas; top price was $6.00.

NOVEMBER 3-7: Ice Capades.

DECEMBER 29: Toronto amateur soccer: Ukraine versus the White Eagles; Olympia-Harmony versus Ulster United. This was the first soccer played at the Gardens, and the first of a number of indoor soccer matches held over the next few years.

1959

JANUARY 26: The Biggest Show of Stars for 1959.

FEBRUARY 2-6: Ice Follies of 1959.

MARCH 22: Timmy's Easter Parade of Stars.

APRIL 19: Allan Cup hockey finals: Vernon Canadians versus Whitby Dunlops.

APRIL 20: Professional world championship tennis. Jack Kramer presented Pancho Gonzales, Lew Hoad, Ashley Cooper and Mal Anderson.

APRIL 28: Benny Goodman and his Orchestra.

MAY 25-30: Metropolitan Opera Company: *Tosca, Carmen, Cavalleria Rusticana, Pagliacci, Die Fledermaus, Rigoletto* and *Madame Butterfly*.

JUNE 11-13: The Bolshoi Ballet, performing highlights from *Giselle* and *Swan Lake*. This was the company's first visit with Ulanova. Top price was $12.50, the highest price paid for seats at the Gardens up to that time.

AUGUST 25-27: Russian Festival of Music and Dance.

SEPTEMBER 21: Dick Clark's Caravan of Stars.

SEPTEMBER 28-OCTOBER 3: Rameses Shrine Circus.

OCTOBER 10: Leafs NHL hockey opener. Toronto beat Chicago 6-3. The opening ceremony was attended by John Diefenbaker, Prime Minister of Canada.

NOVEMBER 9-13: Ice Capades, the twentieth anniversary edition.

NOVEMBER 17: Queensbury Athletic Club boxing: George Chuvalo versus Yvon Durelle. Chuvalo won.

NOVEMBER 22: Boxing on closed circuit television: Floyd Patterson defeated George Chuvalo.

NOVEMBER 26-27: The Polish State Folk Ballet (later to become the Mazowsze Company).

1960

JANUARY 19: International hockey: Moscow All Stars versus Whitby Dunlops.

Beatles' press reception, 1964.
GRAPHIC ARTISTS

Conn Smythe, John Diefenbaker and Colonel W. A. H. MacBrien.
ALEXANDRA STUDIO

Tiny Tim drops the puck between Dave Keon (left) and George Armstrong.
GRAPHIC ARTISTS

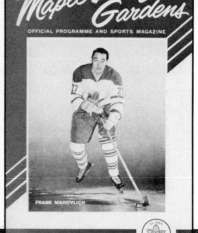

Military band.
GRAPHIC ARTISTS

JANUARY 25: The Biggest Show of Stars for 1960.

FEBRUARY 2-5: Ice Follies of 1960.

FEBRUARY 9: Moscow State Symphony.

FEBRUARY 15: Professional tennis: Pancho Gonzales, Ken Rosewell, Pancho Segura, Tony Trabert.

FEBRUARY 22: Toronto Police Association concert, featuring the Toronto Symphony Orchestra, with Whittemore and Lowe at the piano.

FEBRUARY 23: Fred Waring and his Pennsylvanians.

MARCH 4: Czechoslovakian Olympic hockey team versus Whitby Dunlops. This was the first visit of a Czech team to the Gardens.

MARCH 16-18: Timmy's Easter Parade of Stars, sponsored by the Rotary Club.

APRIL 29: Memorial Cup hockey final: St. Catharines versus Edmonton.

MAY 13-14: Georgian State Dance Company.

MAY 30-JUNE 3: Metropolitan Opera Company: Verdi's *Il Trovatore,* Strauss' *The Gypsy Baron,* Giordano's *Andrea Chenier,* Gounod's *Faust,* Verdi's *Simone Boccanegra* and *La Traviata.*

SEPTEMBER 19: Biggest Show of Stars for 1960.

SEPTEMBER 26-OCTOBER 1: Hamid-Morton Circus for Lions Club charities.

OCTOBER 8: Leafs NHL hockey opener. New York Rangers beat Toronto 5-2. Frank Mahovlich went on to score forty-eight goals this season, a club record. The first puck was dropped by Keiller McKay, Lieutenant-Governor of Ontario.

OCTOBER 12: Count Basie and Stan Kenton concert.

OCTOBER 31: The Biggest Show of Stars for 1960, fall edition. Among the stars were Fabian and Brenda Lee.

NOVEMBER 7-11: Ice Capades.

1961

New publicity offices built during 1961. Harold Ballard, Stafford Smythe and John Bassett take over control of the Gardens from Conn Smythe.

JANUARY 30: Ice Follies of 1961.

MARCH 13: Boxing on closed circuit television: Ingemar Johansson versus Floyd Patterson. This was a first in the building. Via satellite, the Gardens' giant screen was to televise many exciting events from around the world. The arena became a giant theatre, seating double that of the largest theatre in the world. Top ticket price was $10.00.

MARCH 26: Timmy's Easter Parade of Stars for the Easter Seal Campaign and Crippled Children.

APRIL 29: Professional tennis: Jack Kramer presented Pancho Gonzales, Lew Hoad, Andres Gimeno, Alex Olmedo and Barry MacKay.

MAY 26-27: Moiseyev Dance Company.

MAY 30-JUNE 3: Ringling Bros. and Barnum & Bailey Circus. This was the first show at the Gardens to be promoted with the help of Dominion Stores, and from this time on Dominion was to play a large part in many Gardens' events.

JUNE 22: Queensbury Athletic Club wrestling: Dick "Bulldog" Brower defeated Man Mountain Campbell.

JUNE 27: Queensbury Athletic Club boxing: George Chuvalo versus Willi Besmanoff. Chuvalo won by knockout in the fourth round.

JULY 2-6: Kiwanis International convention, the first of the giant conventions in the building.

AUGUST 25-31: Red Army Singers, Dancers and Musicians. Top price was $6.00.

SEPTEMBER 2: Latvian Song Festival.

SEPTEMBER 18: Biggest Show of Stars for 1961, fall edition.

OCTOBER 8: Dick Clark's Caravan of Stars.

OCTOBER 14: Leafs' NHL hockey opener. Toronto beat Boston 3-2. The season was opened by The Right Hon. Louis St. Laurent.

OCTOBER 22-25: Leningrad Kirov Ballet. Top price was $9.00.

NOVEMBER 6-10: Ice Capades.

DECEMBER 4: Boxing: Floyd Patterson versus Tom McNeely.

DECEMBER 12-13: Mazowsze Song and Dance Company.

1962

During 1962, 962 additional seats were added to the Gardens. Kiosks, aisles, and new executive offices were built. The Zamboni ice-cleaning machine made its first appearance.

JANUARY 29-FEBRUARY 2: Ice Follies of 1962.

FEBRUARY 19: Chubby Checker brought the Twist to Toronto fans.

MARCH 21: An Evening with Gershwin.

APRIL 15: Timmy's Easter Parade of Stars for the Easter Seals.

APRIL 25-28: Rotary Ice Revue of 1962.

MAY 25-26: Ukrainian Dance Company.

MAY 27: Rotary musical concert.

MAY 29-JUNE 3: Ringling Bros. and Barnum & Bailey Circus.

SEPTEMBER 4-16: The Moscow Circus. This was the first visit from a European circus. Top price was $4.00.

SEPTEMBER 25: Boxing on closed circuit television: World Heavyweight Championship bout between Floyd Patterson and Sonny Liston. Top price was $6.00. Liston won.

OCTOBER 6: Hockey: NHL All Stars versus The Toronto Maple Leafs.

OCTOBER 13: Leafs NHL hockey opener. Toronto and Boston tied 2-2. Conn Smythe opened the season.

NOVEMBER 5-11: Ice Capades. The Ice Capades was on at 1:30 p.m. and the Leafs played a game at 8:00 that night, showing just how quickly the Gardens could be converted.

NOVEMBER 20: Royal Scots Guards and Argyll and Sutherland Highlanders.

NOVEMBER 23: International hockey: Russians versus All Stars.

DECEMBER 10-13: Bolshoi Ballet, performing *Chopiniana, Walpurgis Nacht, Ballet School, Swan Lake, Bayaderka, Gayane* and *Divertissements.*

1963

Hot Stove Club built during 1963, the first private club in the NHL. Its name was inspired by the old Hot Stove League.

JANUARY 24: Queensbury Athletic Club wrestling: World Title match between Lou Thesz and Buddy Rogers. Thesz won.

JANUARY 25: Telegram-Maple Leaf Indoor Games. Because of the popularity of two Canadian runners, Bruce Kidd and Bill Crothers, the Gardens instituted an annual track meet directed by Ken Twigg.

JANUARY 28-FEBRUARY 2: Ice Follies of 1963.

FEBRUARY 11: Exhibition hockey: Trail Smoke Eaters versus the Eastern University All Stars. The Trail team was on its way to the world championships in Europe.

FEBRUARY 25: Professional tennis: Ken Rosewall, Andres Gimeno, Earl Bucholz, Rod Laver, Barry MacKay and Luis Ayala.

MARCH 29: New Democratic Party political rally.

APRIL 1: Timmy's Easter Parade of Stars.

JUNE 1: Diocesan Eucharistic Day Mass.

JULY 9: Tommy Dorsey's Orchestra.

JULY 19: The Dick Clark Show.

JULY 22: Boxing on closed circuit television: Floyd Patterson versus Sonny Liston. Patterson was knocked out in the first round.

AUGUST 13: World Anglican Congress, with the Archbishop of Canterbury.

AUGUST 18: Anglican Missionary rally service.

AUGUST 31: Country music show.

SEPTEMBER 17: Black Watch Band.

SEPTEMBER 30-OCTOBER 6: Don Ameche's International Showtime Circus.

OCTOBER 12: Leafs NHL hockey opener. Toronto 5, Boston 1. The season was opened by Prime Minister Lester Pearson.

OCTOBER 18: Hootenanny.

NOVEMBER 5-12: Ice Capades.

NOVEMBER 21-22: Olympic figure skating trials.

NOVEMBER 24-29: Canadian Championship Rodeo.

DECEMBER 29: International hockey: Swedish National Team versus Canadian National Team.

1964

Track floor built during 1964 at a cost of over $25,000.

JANUARY 1-4: Tournament of Champions Indoor Curling Bonspiel.

JANUARY 5: International hockey: Swedish National Team versus Czechoslovakian National Team.

JANUARY 24: Telegram-Maple Leaf Indoor Games.

JANUARY 27-FEBRUARY 2: Ice Follies of 1964.

FEBRUARY 25: Boxing on closed circuit television: Sonny Liston versus Cassius Clay. Top price was $7.50. Clay defeated Liston to take the World Title.

MARCH 2: Mazowsze, the Polish Song and Dance Company.

MARCH 16: Timmy's Easter Parade of Stars.

APRIL 25: The Leafs beat the Detroit Red Wings 4-0 to win the Stanley Cup, four games to three.

MAY 2: Greek Community of Metropolitan Toronto church service.

MAY 3: Memorial Cup hockey playoffs: Toronto Marlboros versus the Edmonton Oil Kings.

MAY 12-15: The Lipizzaner Horses of the Spanish Riding School from Vienna, led into the ring by Ambassador E. Leitner.

MAY 16: Estonian Festival.

MAY 27-31: Ringling Bros. and Barnum & Bailey Circus.

JUNE 7-11: Rotary International convention.

JULY 8-11: Lions Club International convention with plenary sessions, a Kansas Night show and an International Night show.

SEPTEMBER 7: The Beatles. Shows at 4 p.m. and 8:30 p.m. Top price was $5.50.

SEPTEMBER 19: Hockey: NHL pre-season game, the first between NHL opponents at the Gardens.

SEPTEMBER 27: Mina and Pargi, Italian singers, presented by Johnny Lombardi.

SEPTEMBER 29-OCTOBER 4: The Wonderful World of Sports, with narrator Quentin Reynolds.

OCTOBER 5: Lacrosse: Jim Smith Benefit Night.

OCTOBER 8: Ireland on Parade.

OCTOBER 10: NHL All Star game: Toronto versus the NHL All Stars.

OCTOBER 17: Leafs NHL hockey opener: Toronto 7, Boston 2. The Hon. W. Earl Rowe, Lieutenant-Governor of Ontario, opened the season.

OCTOBER 25: Rita Pavone.

OCTOBER 29: The Royal Irish Brigade military tattoo.

NOVEMBER 1: Gerry and the Pacemakers.

NOVEMBER 2: The Dave Clark Five.

NOVEMBER 22-27: Canadian Championship Rodeo.

DECEMBER 1-8: Ice Capades.

DECEMBER 13: International hockey: Russia versus Canada.

1965

Hot Stove Club expanded in 1965, more seats put in the Gardens, new press box built on the east side.

JANUARY 3: Frank Tunney's pro wrestling: Johnny Valentine versus The Sheik. This was the first fight for The Sheik at the Gardens. Valentine defeated him.

JANUARY 5-8: The Curling Tournament of Champions.

JANUARY 10: International hockey: Czechoslovakia versus Canada.

JANUARY 29: Telegram-Maple Leaf Indoor Games.

FEBRUARY 1: Boxing on closed circuit television: Floyd Patterson versus George Chuvalo. Patterson won.

FEBRUARY 11: Frank Tunney's pro wrestling; Johnny Valentine defeated Bulldog Brower; Whipper Billy Watson versus The Sheik. The Sheik did not appear again at the Gardens until 1969.

FEBRUARY 28: Exhibition hockey: NHL Oldtimers versus Canada.

MARCH 12: World Figure Skaters' Tour of 1965.

MARCH 14: Rita Pavone.

MARCH 18: Claudio Villa.

APRIL 24: Greek church service.

APRIL 25: The Rolling Stones.

APRIL 26: Canadian Girls in Training (CGIT) pageant.

MAY 2-8: Six-day bicycle races.

MAY 11-13: Moiseyev Ballet.

MAY 16: International Variety Show, sponsored by Johnny Lombardi. The performers were Piccola, Pupa, Giorgio Consoloini, Bobby Curtola, the Camillo Family, Bobby Vinci and Enzina Bliti.

MAY 23: Emilio Mascia and Associates present Remo Germani, Nicola di Bari, Narciso Parigi and Roberta Mazzoni.

MAY 25: Boxing on closed circuit television: Muhammad Ali versus Sonny Liston. Ali won.

MAY 29-30: Latvian Song Festival.

JUNE 2-6: Ringling Bros. and Barnum & Bailey Circus.

JUNE 8-10: The Royal Ballet with Rudolf Nureyev. The troupe performed *Swan Lake*, *The Dream*, *Les Patineurs*, *La Bayadere* and *Giselle*.

JULY 2-4: Alcoholics Anonymous convention.

AUGUST 17: The Beatles.

SEPTEMBER 5: The Beach Boys, with Sonny and Cher as the opening act.

SEPTEMBER 18-19: Royal Marines Tattoo.

OCTOBER 22: International volleyball: USA versus USSR.

OCTOBER 23: Leafs NHL hockey opener: Chicago beat Toronto 4-0. The season was opened by Frederick G. Gardiner, Q.C.

OCTOBER 31: The Rolling Stones.

NOVEMBER 1: Boxing: George Chuvalo versus Ernie Terrell. The best seats cost $50.00, the highest at the Gardens to that time.

NOVEMBER 4: New Democratic Party rally.

NOVEMBER 22: Boxing on closed circuit television: Muhammad Ali versus Floyd Patterson. Ali won.

DECEMBER 7-12: Ice Capades.

DECEMBER 14: International hockey: Russia versus Toronto Marlboros.

1966

North and south mezzanine galleries built in 1966, extra red seats added, new directors' room built, new television lights and a new grille added.

JANUARY 5: International hockey: Sweden versus Toronto Marlboros.

JANUARY 9: International hockey: Czechoslovakia versus Canada.

JANUARY 11-14: Tournament of Champions Curling Bonspiel.

JANUARY 30: Frank Tunney's pro wrestling: Bruno Sammartino versus Professor Hiro.

FEBRUARY 1-6: Shipstads and Johnson Ice Follies.

FEBRUARY 20-22: Hungarian Dance Company.

FEBRUARY 23: Toronto Police Association concert. Seiji Ozawa conducted the Toronto Symphony Orchestra, with Whittemore and Lowe at the piano.

FEBRUARY 25: Telegram-Maple Leaf Indoor Games.

MARCH 6: American Hockey League: Rochester versus Hershey. Rochester used the Gardens as a home base until May due to a bowling tournament in their arena.

MARCH 29: Boxing: World Heavyweight Championship bout between Muhammad Ali and George Chuvalo. Top seat price was $100, the highest ever at the Gardens. Ali won a slugfest.

APRIL 9: Greek Community of Metropolitan Toronto church service.

MAY 4: Memorial Cup hockey playoff: Oshawa versus Edmonton. Bobby Orr was a star for Oshawa.

MAY 8: Johnny Morandi and Little Tony and his Group in concert.

MAY 30: Auto racing on closed circuit television: Indianapolis 500.

JUNE 29: The Rolling Stones.

AUGUST 17: The Beatles.

SEPTEMBER 24: The Toronto Sound: fourteen Canadian bands.

OCTOBER 1: Poland's Millenium of Christianity celebration.

OCTOBER 22: Leafs NHL hockey opener. New York Rangers and Toronto Maple Leafs tied 4-4. Ontario premier John P. Robarts dropped the first puck.

NOVEMBER 6-7: Ukrainian Dance Company.

NOVEMBER 8-13: Ice Capades. This was the first time that Saturday night, a traditional home date for the Toronto Maple Leafs, was surrendered to another attraction.

NOVEMBER 14: Boxing on closed circuit television: Muhammad Ali versus Cleveland Williams. Ali won by technical knockout to retain the World Title.

NOVEMBER 17: Frank Tunney's pro wrestling: a six-man tag-team match.

NOVEMBER 20: The Beach Boys.

NOVEMBER 24-25: Royal Highland Fusiliers.

DECEMBER 28: At 10:30 a.m. a Dominion Stores Leaf practice; at 8 p.m. international hockey, the Czechoslovakian National Team versus the Junior All Stars.

1967

A new press room was built in 1967 close to the east press box. Mezzanine seating was completed, as were concessions, a new Marlboro dressing room and a programme room.

JANUARY 10: International hockey: Canada versus Russia.

JANUARY 31-FEBRUARY 5: Ice Follies.

FEBRUARY 6: Boxing: World Heavyweight Championship between Muhammad Ali and Ernie Terrell on closed circuit, with Ali the winner.

FEBRUARY 21: Toronto Police Association concert, with soloist Lois Marshall.

FEBRUARY 24: Telegram-Maple Leaf Centennial Games.

MARCH 9: Oldtimers hockey: Detroit versus Toronto.

MARCH 12: Italian Chiama San Remo 1967.

APRIL 2: The Monkees.

APRIL 9: The Andy Williams Show, with Henry Mancini and his forty-piece orchestra.

APRIL 29: Greek church service.

MAY 2: Leafs win the Stanley Cup, beating Montreal four games to two. It was the first time the Leafs had played in May, and the last time they won the Stanley Cup.

MAY 16: Ontario Folk Arts Festival, with guest Her Royal Highness Princess Alexandra of Kent.

MAY 22: Centennial Cool-Out: The Staccatos, The Guess Who, The Power, M.G. and the Escorts, The Happenings, and Tommy James and the Shondells.

JULY 1: The Mamas and the Papas.

AUGUST 2: Israeli Philharmonic Orchestra. Top price was $10.00.

AUGUST 9: Herman's Hermits.

AUGUST 13-19: Bolshoi Ballet, performing *Don Quixote, Giselle, Swan Lake,* Act II, *Highlight Programme#2,* and *Prince Igor,* Act II.

AUGUST 20: Herb Alpert and the Tijuana Brass.

SEPTEMBER 7-9: Progressive Conservative political rally, a most dramatic convention at which John Diefenbaker was defeated and Robert Stanfield elected national leader of the party.

SEPTEMBER 17: Dominico Modugno (Mr. Volare).

SEPTEMBER 19: Telephone Pioneers of America stage show.

SEPTEMBER 26-OCTOBER 1: Moscow Circus.

OCTOBER 8: Italian show: Nino Tarranto and his Company.

OCTOBER 13-15: Welsh and Scots Guards bands.

OCTOBER 14: NHL hockey opener for the Leafs. Opening ceremonies were performed by the Hon. Robert Stanfield.

OCTOBER 25: The NHL had expanded to twelve teams during the summer. On this date the Leafs played the Los Angeles Kings, the first expansion team to play in the building.

OCTOBER 27: United Appeal Gardens party.

OCTOBER 29: Italian show: Little Tony and Narciso Parigi.

NOVEMBER 6-12: Ice Capades. There were three shows on Saturday for the first time.

NOVEMBER 19: James Brown.

1968

New upholstered individual grey and green seats built in 1968 at a cost of over $250,000.

An alphalite (moving) message board was constructed, the first in North America. Capacity of the building increased to 16,307 seats for hockey.

JANUARY 7: Hockey: Italian National Team versus Canadian Italian team.

JANUARY 16: Hockey: NHL All Stars versus the Toronto Maple Leafs. The All Star Game was now played at mid-season.

JANUARY 21: Italian show featuring Caterina Cabelli and her group.

JANUARY 30-FEBRUARY 11: Ice Follies.

MARCH 1: Telegram-Maple Leaf Indoor Games, 1968 Olympic edition.

MARCH 4: Boxing on closed circuit television: Joe Frazier versus Mathis; Nino Benvenuti versus Archie Griffith. Frazier knocked out Mathis in the eleventh round; Benvenuti defeated Griffith to regain the World Middleweight Title.

MARCH 5: Toronto Police Association concert, with Eleanor Calbes and the Buffalo Philharmonic Orchestra under the direction of Lukas Foss.

MARCH 10: Italian show with Alfred Tucci.

MARCH 17: The Greatest All-British Revue, starring Vera Lynn, Mrs. Mills and the Irish Rovers.

APRIL 7: James Brown.

APRIL 19: Calypso Festival.

APRIL 20: Greek church service.

APRIL 21: Oldtimers hockey: The Leafs versus the Montreal Canadiens, with all proceeds to the Charlie Conacher Cancer Research Fund.

MAY 1-5: Soviet Navy Ensemble.

MAY 11: Italian variety show, a benefit performance for the Canadian Save the Children Fund, with a special appearance by Nino Benvenuti.

MAY 8: Professional lacrosse: Toronto versus Detroit.

JUNE 30-JULY 3: Kiwanis International convention.

JULY 14: Frank Tunney's pro wrestling: Bulldog Brower versus The Assassin.

SEPTEMBER 9: Ford Motor Company display.

OCTOBER 4: The Greatest British Variety Show, starring Anne Shelton, Mrs. Mills, Dainty and Lowe and David Whitfield.

OCTOBER 16: Leafs NHL hockey opener; Toronto versus Pittsburgh. Pittsburgh was the first expansion team to open the season at the Gardens. Hon. William Davis, Minister of Education for Ontario, officiated at the opening. Jim Dorey had nine penalties totalling forty-eight minutes, both club records.

OCTOBER 27: Italian show, featuring Giani Morandi.

NOVEMBER 1: The Young Rascals and The Union Gap.

NOVEMBER 4-11: Ice Capades.

NOVEMBER 15: James Brown.

NOVEMBER 16: Watchtower religious meeting.

1969

George Mara installed as President of Maple Leaf Gardens in 1969. New offices and a second alphalite arena board built.

JANUARY 19: International hockey: Canada versus Russia.

JANUARY 21-FEBRUARY 2: Ice Follies, starring Richard Dwyer, Mr. Frick and Donald Jackson.

FEBRUARY 14: The 7th Annual Telegram-Maple Leaf Indoor Games.

MARCH 21: The Doors concert.

MARCH 23: 1969 World Figure Skating Champions exhibition.

MARCH 28: 48th Highlanders Military Tattoo.

APRIL 12: Greek Community of Metropolitan Toronto church service.

APRIL 27: Paul Mauriat and his Orchestra.

MAY 3: The Jimi Hendrix Experience.

MAY 7-11: Russian Festival of song, dance and music.

JUNE 12-13: International floor hockey tournament for the Retarded Children's Olympics.

JUNE 15: Metro Toronto Concert for Timmy.

JUNE 20: James Brown.

OCTOBER 2-4: British Tournament and Tattoo.

OCTOBER 6: Frank Tunney's amateur boxing: Canadian amateur team versus the Italian amateur team.

OCTOBER 12: Italian variety show with Rita Pavone.

OCTOBER 15: NHL opening hockey game for the Leafs. Montreal tied Toronto 2-2, with Foster Hewitt dropping the puck for the ceremonial face-off.

OCTOBER 26: Italian variety show, featuring Nino Taranto and his Company and Al Bano and his Group.

OCTOBER 30: Herb Alpert and the Tijuana Brass, with guest O. C. Smith.

NOVEMBER 3-9: Ice Capades.

NOVEMBER 10: The Johnny Cash Show.

NOVEMBER 16: The Vera Lynn Show.

NOVEMBER 28: Engelbert Humperdinck. Top price was $10.00.

DECEMBER 4, 5, 7: Osipov Balalaika Orchestra.

DECEMBER 26: International hockey: Canada versus Russia.

1970

New red seats installed in 1970, an office built for Conn Smythe, Stafford Smythe was back as President, and the Leafs dressing room expanded. A new $20,000 incinerator built to solve pollution problems.

JANUARY 1: International hockey: Canada versus Czechoslovakia.

JANUARY 20-FEBRUARY 1: Ice Follies.

FEBRUARY 5: The 8th Annual Telegram-Maple Leaf Indoor Games.

FEBRUARY 16: Boxing on closed circuit television: World Heavyweight Boxing Championship between Joe Frazier and Jimmy Ellis. Frazier won.

MARCH 1: Buck Owens and the Buckaroos.

RIGHT: *Gymnast Karen Kelsall.*
ONTARIO SPORTSCENE

Ontario Invitational Floor Hockey Tournament for the Mentally Retarded, 1974, with Pierre Elliott Trudeau throwing the ring.
GRAPHIC ARTISTS

Billy Graham signs autographs before his 1978 crusade.
JEFF GOODE

David Bowie.
PETER CORIGLIONE

MARCH 6: Toronto Police Association concert with the Toronto Symphony Orchestra under the direction of Arthur Fiedler, with guest pianist Ronald Turini.

MARCH 13: England, Ireland and Scotland in Concert, featuring Frankie Vaughan, Kenneth McKellar, The Dubliners, 48th Highlanders and the Butler Irish School of Dancing.

MARCH 19-30: Disney on Parade.

APRIL 3: Delaney, Bonny and Friends.

APRIL 25: Greek church service.

MAY 3: Ontario Seconday School Teachers' Federation.

MAY 10: Frank Tunney's pro wrestling: The Sheik versus Haystack Calhoun. The Sheik won, attacking Calhoun with part of the turnbuckle.

MAY 15-18: Garden Bros. Circus.

JUNE 1-7: Red Army Singers, Dancers and Musicians.

JUNE 11: Tom Jones. Top price was $12.50.

JUNE 14: World Cup Soccer on closed circuit television: Italy versus Brazil.

JUNE 28-30: Moiseyev Dance Company.

JULY 4: Latvian Song Festival.

JULY 31: Caribana Extravaganza '70 with Johnny Nash.

AUGUST 4: Boxing on closed circuit television: George Chuvalo versus George Foreman. Foreman won by technical knockout.

SEPTEMBER 19: Creedence Clearwater Revival.

SEPTEMBER 26-27: Coldstream Guards and The Black Watch with the Massed Bands, Pipes, Drums and Dancers.

OCTOBER 4: Sly and the Family Stone.

OCTOBER 6-12: Moscow Circus on Ice.

OCTOBER 14: Leafs NHL hockey opening game: Leafs beat St. Louis 7-3. Clarence Campbell, the President of the National Hockey League, opened the season.

OCTOBER 16: Blood, Sweat and Tears.

OCTOBER 26: Boxing on closed circuit television: Muhammad Ali versus Jerry Quarry. Ali won.

NOVEMBER 3-8: Ice Capades.

NOVEMBER 26, 27, 29: Royal Lipizzan Stallions.

DECEMBER 7: Boxing on closed circuit television: Muhammad Ali versus Oscar Bonavena. Ali knocked out Bonavena.

DECEMBER 23: NHL hockey: Toronto Maple Leafs versus Vancouver Canucks. Vancouver was the first new team into the building after the second NHL expansion.

DECEMBER 28: Hockey Canada's Intercollegiate Invitational Tournament: University of Calgary versus Laurentian University; University of Toronto versus York University.

1971

JANUARY 14: NBA basketball: Cincinnati Royals versus Los Angeles Lakers. Pro basketball was tried at the Gardens as an experiment; it was successful, but there hasn't been enough interest for a Toronto team.

JANUARY 19-31: Ice Follies.

FEBRUARY 1: Chicago concert.

FEBRUARY 5: The 9th Annual Telegram-Maple Leaf Indoor Games.

FEBRUARY 7: Mazowsze, Polish Song and Dance Company.

FEBRUARY 11-12: Progressive Conservative Party convention.

FEBRUARY 19: Oldtimers hockey: Toronto versus Montreal, with proceeds to the Charlie Conacher Cancer Research Fund.

FEBRUARY 26: Toronto Police Association concert: Toronto Symphony Orchestra under the direction of Alfredo Antonini, with guest soloist soprano Nadja Witkowska.

MARCH 7: Roller Derby: The San Francisco Bombers versus The Midwest Pioneers.

MARCH 8: Boxing on closed circuit television: Donato Paduano versus Clyde Gray; Muhammad Ali versus Joe Frazier. Frazier defeated Ali. Top price was $20.00.

MAY 10: Boxing: George Chuvalo versus Jimmy Ellis, with Ellis the winner. Foreman and Peralta were seen on closed circuit television.

MAY 13-16: Garden Bros. Circus.

MAY 21-23: Georgian State Song and Dance Ensemble.

MAY 24: Filming of the motion picture *Face Off*.

MAY 28: 48th Highlanders Tattoo.

MAY 29: Tom Jones.

MAY 30: Rock variety show: Cheap Thrills II, Sly and the Family Stone, James Gang, Buddy Miles, Taj Mahal.

JUNE 4-6: Antique show and sale.

JUNE 9-10: International Floor Hockey Tournament for the Retarded Children's Olympics.

AUGUST 7-8: A Canine Extravaganza: All-Breed Dog show.

SEPTEMBER 1: Harold Ballard and Stafford Smythe buy out John Bassett for $5,700,000.

SEPTEMBER 4: Led Zeppelin.

OCTOBER 1-3: Royal Lipizzan Stallions.

OCTOBER 9: Grand Funk Railroad.

OCTOBER 10: Italian show, featuring Nicola De Bari and Nino Taranto.

OCTOBER 13: Leafs NHL hockey opener: the Detroit Red Wings beat the Leafs 5-3. Clarence "Hap" Day and thirteen other members of the 1931-32 Stanley Cup team performed the official opening honours at this fortieth anniversary game.

NOVEMBER 2-7: Ice Capades.

DECEMBER 2: NBA basketball: Baltimore Bullets versus Buffalo Braves.

DECEMBER 3: Ike and Tina Turner Revue.

DECEMBER 7: Roller Derby: San Francisco Bombers versus Canadian Chiefs.

DECEMBER 9: The Faces, featuring Rod Stewart.

1972

JANUARY 9: Frank Tunney's pro wrestling: The Sheik versus Bulldog Brower.

JANUARY 14: ABA basketball: Indiana Pacers versus Memphis Kings; Kentucky Colonels versus Dallas Chaparrals.

JANUARY 18-30: Ice Follies.

FEBRUARY 4: Toronto Star-Maple Leaf Indoor Games. Sponsorship had switched from the Toronto Telegram.

FEBRUARY 7: Harold Ballard buys the late Stafford Smythe's share of the Gardens for $7,500,000.

FEBRUARY 13: Three Dog Night.

FEBRUARY 25: Toronto Police Association concert, with Ron Goodwin conducting the Toronto Symphony Orchestra.

MARCH 18: Tour of Champions: Exhibition of figure skating champions from around the world.

MARCH 28: Moody Blues.

APRIL 13: Timmy Tyke hockey tournament.

APRIL 5: Joe Cocker.

APRIL 10: The Regimental Band, Pipes, Drums and Dancers of Her Majesty's Scots Guards.

APRIL 19: European Cup Soccer on closed circuit television: Glasgow Celtic versus Inter Milan.

APRIL 21: Rock and Roll Revival, with Little Richard, Chubby Checker, Danny and the Juniors, The Shirells, Gary U.S. Bonds, The Five Satins, The Coasters and Bobby Comstock.

APRIL 29: European Cup Soccer on closed circuit television: Italy versus Belgium; England versus West Germany.

MAY 13: European Cup Soccer on closed circuit television: England versus West Germany; Belgium versus Italy.

MAY 31: Championship Soccer on closed circuit television: Ajax versus Inter Milan.

JUNE 4: Jethro Tull.

JUNE 26: Cheap Thrills, featuring Edgar Winter and Humble Pie.

JULY 15: The Rolling Stones and Stevie Wonder.

AUGUST 22: International hockey: Team Canada Whites versus Team Canada Reds. Harold Ballard allowed the Gardens to be used as a training site for Team Canada before its series with the USSR.

SEPTEMBER 4: Team Canada beat the USSR 4-1 in one of the greatest hockey games at the Gardens.

SEPTEMBER 7: The Faces, featuring Rod Stewart.

SEPTEMBER 19: United Appeal gala.

SEPTEMBER 26: Ten Years After concert, with Edgar Winter and Peter Frampton.

SEPTEMBER 28: The Dukla, Ukrainian Dance Company.

OCTOBER 5: Elton John.

OCTOBER 6: Roller Derby: New York State versus Ontario Royals.

OCTOBER 7: Leafs NHL opening game. Chicago beat Toronto 3-1. King Clancy dropped the puck.

OCTOBER 8: Festival Italiano.

OCTOBER 17: Liberal Party rally, with entertainment provided by the Optimist Band, Crowbar and The Travellers.

OCTOBER 20: Rock and Roll Revival.

OCTOBER 27: Roller Derby: Ontario Royals versus Ohio All Stars.

OCTOBER 31: Yes concert, with J. Geils Band.

NOVEMBER 3: Carabinieri, the continental band of Rome.

NOVEMBER 8-13: Ice Capades.

NOVEMBER 21: Boxing: a live card including Oscar "Ringo" Dealecio versus Julie Madel and Clyde Gray versus Otho Thyson. On closed circuit television, Muhammad Ali knocked out Bob Foster; Joe "King" Roman versus Terry Daniels; Ken Norton versus Jack O'Halloran.

DECEMBER 29: International hockey: USSR versus Czechoslovakia.

1973

Harold Ballard back as President of Maple Leaf Gardens in 1973. Concert Productions International formed to bring modern music to the Gardens.

JANUARY 15: Neil Young. He was the first Torontonian, not a religious figure, to fill the Gardens to its 18,000-person capacity.

JANUARY 16-28: Ice Follies, starring Richard Dwyer, Mr. Frick and Donald Jackson.

JANUARY 22: Boxing on closed circuit television: World Heavyweight Championship between Joe Frazier and George Foreman. Top price was $12.00. Foreman won.

JANUARY 29: Toronto Indoor Soccer League: Toronto Canadians versus Toronto Italia; Toronto Portugese versus Toronto British.

FEBRUARY 2: Toronto Star-Maple Leaf Indoor Games.

FEBRUARY 5: Toronto Indoor Soccer League: Toronto Italia versus Toronto Portugese; Toronto British versus Toronto Canadians.

FEBRUARY 12: Boxing: Clyde Gray versus Eddie Blay for the Commonwealth Welterweight Title; Al Sparks versus Gary Summerhays for the Canadian Light Heavyweight Championship. Top price was $15.00. Gray and Summerhays won.

FEBRUARY 20: Santana.

FEBRUARY 25: Mazowsze Dance Company.

MARCH 2: Toronto Police Association concert, with Arthur Fiedler conducting the Toronto Symphony Orchestra.

MARCH 11: Pink Floyd.

MARCH 30: Liza Minelli in concert with Desi Arnaz, Jr. There was also a celebrity tennis match staged in conjunction with this concert.

APRIL 1: Festival Italiano with Gianni Morandi and Iva Zanicchi.

APRIL 2: Timmy Tyke Tournament.

APRIL 10: Hockey: WHA playoffs, Ottawa Nationals versus New England Whalers. This was the first time the WHA had played in the building.

APRIL 13: Rock concert: BBA, Paul Butterfield, Wet Willie.

MAY 4: Frank Zappa and the Mothers of Invention.

MAY 6: Ukrainian Catholic Council.

MAY 11: International Track Association Professional Indoor Games.

MAY 19: Rock and Roll Revival III, with Fabian, Dion and the Belmonts, Bill Haley and the Comets and The Chiffons.

MAY 26: Roller Derby.

MAY 30: Jethro Tull.

JUNE 8: The Donna Fargo Show, with Hank Williams, Jr. and The Cheating Hearts, Lamar Morris, The Charlie Rich Show, Tommy Overstreet and The Nashville Experiment, Susan St. Marie, Jan Howard, The Myres Brothers and the Jubilaires.

JUNE 24: Frank Tunney's pro wrestling: Harley Race versus Pat O'Connor for the World Title, The Shiek versus Abdullah Farouk. Race won the World Title.

JUNE 28: The British are Coming: Herman's Hermits, Gerry and the Pacemakers, The Shondells, Wayne Fontana and the Mindbenders, Billy J. Kramer.

AUGUST 13-24: General Motors 1974 New Model Presentation.

AUGUST 29: Carlos Santana, John McLaughlin and the Mahavishnu.

SEPTEMBER 10: Boxing on closed circuit television: Muhammad Ali versus Ken Norton. Ali won by decision.

SEPTEMBER 22: Boxing: World Welterweight Championship, José Napoles defeated Clyde Gray. First match in the "Fight A Month" Series. Top price was $50.00.

SEPTEMBER 23: Wrestling: Jack Brisco versus Eric the Animal.

OCTOBER 4: NBA basketball: Buffalo Braves versus Milwaukee Bucks.

OCTOBER 5: Roller Derby.

OCTOBER 7: Johnny Lombardi's Festival Italiano.

OCTOBER 10: Leafs NHL hockey opener: Toronto beat Buffalo 7-4. In honour of the two Swedish players who had joined the team, Borje Salming and Inge Hammarstrom, Swedish Ambassador Ake Malmaeus was invited to open the season. Top seats were $7.70.

OCTOBER 11: Boxing: Light Heavyweight Championship bout between Ken Buchanan and Frankie Otero. Buchanan won.

OCTOBER 21: Roller Derby: Canadian All Stars versus Brooklyn Bombers.

OCTOBER 26: NBA Basketball: Buffalo Braves versus Cleveland Cavaliers.

NOVEMBER 2: The Johnny Cash Show.

NOVEMBER 4: Festival and church service of the Ukrainian World Congress; NBA basketball: Buffalo Braves versus Chicago Bullets.

NOVEMBER 5: The Edgar Winter Group.

NOVEMBER 6: Roller Derby: Canadian All Stars versus Brooklyn Bombers.

NOVEMBER 13-18: Ice Capades, starring Karen Magnussen.

DECEMBER 5: Roller Derby: Canadian All Stars versus Chicago Hawks.

DECEMBER 7: Emerson, Lake and Palmer.

DECEMBER 9: NBA basketball: Buffalo Braves versus Boston Celtics.

DECEMBER 10: Krasnoiarsk: Siberian Dance Ensemble.

DECEMBER 14: Alice Cooper.

DECEMBER 16: Whipper Billy Watson's Christmas Skate for Timmy.

DECEMBER 23: NBA basketball: Buffalo Braves versus Capitol Bullets.

DECEMBER 27: Leaf practice sponsored by The Bank of Nova Scotia and Mattel Canada; CCM International Hockey Tournament: Sweden versus the Toronto Marlboros.

DECEMBER 31: Winter Pop IV, with Seals and Crofts, Crowbar, The Stampeders, England Dan and John Ford Colley, The Grease Ball Boogie Band.

1974

Red seats turned into golds and blues into reds in 1974. New additions were made to dressing rooms, and a dressing room built for the Toronto Toros of the WHA.

JANUARY 1-8: CCM International Hockey Tournament.

JANUARY 6: NBA basketball: Buffalo Braves versus Atlanta Hawks.

JANUARY 10: Bob Dylan and The Band.

JANUARY 15-27: Ice Follies.

JANUARY 28: Boxing: All Canada Sports closed circuit bout between Muhammad Ali and Joe Frazier. Ali won.

FEBRUARY 3: Basketball: Israeli National Team versus University of Waterloo Warriors; Buffalo Braves versus Philadelphia 76rs.

FEBRUARY 7: Indoor soccer: North American Soccer League All Stars versus Moscow Red Army.

FEBRUARY 8: Roller Derby: New York Chiefs versus Canadian All Stars.

FEBRUARY 13: World Cup Soccer on closed circuit television: Spain versus Yugoslavia.

FEBRUARY 15: Toronto Star-Maple Leaf Indoor Games.

FEBRUARY 18: Boxing: Clyde Gray versus Bunny Grant for the Commonwealth Championship. Gray won.

FEBRUARY 22: Yes concert.

FEBRUARY 26: World Cup Soccer on closed circuit television: West Germany versus Italy. A junior international hockey game was also played on this date: Markham Royalls versus Soviet Army Midgets.

MARCH 1: Toronto Police Association concert: Ron Goodwin conducting the Toronto Symphony Orchestra.

MARCH 11: Johnny Winter.

MARCH 12: Big Band Cavalcade: Bob Crosby, Freddy Martin, George Shearing, Margaret Whiting.

MARCH 13: International volleyball: Japan, Korea, Canada.

MARCH 16: Roller Derby: Baltimore Cats versus Canadian All Stars.

MARCH 19-24: Peter Pan.

MARCH 26: Boxing on closed circuit television: World Heavyweight Championship between George Foreman and Ken Norton. Foreman won by knockout, retaining the World Heavyweight Title.

APRIL 5: The Guess Who.

APRIL 7: WHA hockey playoffs: Toronto Toros versus Cleveland Crusaders for the Avco Cup.

MAY 3-4: *Time to Run*: A film presented by World Wide Pictures.

MAY 21: Lacrosse: Toronto Tomahawks versus Les Québécois.

MAY 24-25: Ontario Invitational Floor Hockey Tournament for the Mentally Retarded.

JUNE 12: Olympic gymnastics: Russia versus Canada.

JUNE 13-16, 18, JULY 3, 19, 22, 23: World Cup Soccer on closed circuit television.

JUNE 17: Boxing on closed circuit television: Joe Frazier versus Jerry Quarry, with Frazier winning, plus a live bout between Clyde Gray and Gil King.

JUNE 26: International basketball: Mainland China versus Canada; Italy versus George Brown College.

JULY 21: Tae-Kwon-Do (Korean Art of Self-Defence).

AUGUST 21-30: General Motors 1975 New Model Presentation.

SEPTEMBER 8: Closed circuit television of Evel Knievel's Snake River Canyon jump.

SEPTEMBER 10-15: Ukrainian Festival on Ice.

SEPTEMBER 19: International hockey: Canada versus Russia. Canada won 4-1. Top ticket price was $12.00, and the biggest hockey gate to that time was realized, nearly $200,000.

SEPTEMBER 26: NBA basketball: Buffalo Braves versus Detroit Pistons.

SEPTEMBER 28: Welsh Guards and the Argyll and Sutherland Highlanders.

SEPTEMBER 29: Slask, Polish Song and Dance Company.

OCTOBER 2: Eric Clapton.

OCTOBER 7: Rick Wakeman.

OCTOBER 9: Leafs NHL opener versus the Kansas City Scouts. Gordon Sinclair opened the season. Tickets were $12.00 tops.

OCTOBER 15: WHA opener for the Toros. Toronto versus New England Whalers. Top price was $9.00.

OCTOBER 21: Van Morrison.

OCTOBER 29: Boxing on closed circuit television: World Heavyweight Championship between Muhammad Ali and George Foreman. The best seats went for $25.00. Ali knocked out Foreman, and regained the World Heavyweight Title.

OCTOBER 30: Roller Derby: Canadian All Stars versus California Thunderbirds.

NOVEMBER 5: World Gymnastics: Milk Meet '74.

NOVEMBER 7-17: Ice Capades. The show grossed $600,000 for sixteen shows, a new high for the building.

NOVEMBER 18: Elton John.

DECEMBER 6: George Harrison with Ravi Shankar.

DECEMBER 16: Genesis.

DECEMBER 20: Whipper Billy Watson Skate for Timmy.

DECEMBER 26: International hockey: Toronto Marlboros versus Czechoslovakia.

1975

New arborite boards installed in July and August of 1975.

JANUARY 2: International hockey: Toronto Marlboros versus USSR.

JANUARY 14-26: Ice Follies. Previous gross record for ice shows broken.

JANUARY 27: J. Geils Band.

FEBRUARY 6: Cookie Gilchrist presented Marvin Gaye, Ike and Tina Turner, and Tavares.

FEBRUARY 9: International hockey: Toronto Marlboros versus the Japanese National Team, won by the Marlies 6-5. The backers of Japanese hockey, the Tsutsumi brothers, liked the game and the Toronto Maple Leafs so much that they chose Toronto as the city in Canada to build one of their Prince hotels.

FEBRUARY 14: Toronto Star-Maple Leaf Indoor Games.

FEBRUARY 28: Toronto Police Association concert, the fifty-sixth edition, featuring Victor Feldbrill with the Toronto Symphony Orchestra and guest soloist Jacqueline Gooderham.

MARCH 18: Stevie Wonder.

MARCH 29: World Figure Skating Tour.

MARCH 31: Timmy Tyke Hockey Tournament.

APRIL 3: Johnny Winter.

APRIL 8: Hockey on closed circuit television: playoff game between Toronto Maple Leafs and Los Angeles Kings.

APRIL 11: Jehovah's Witnesses religious meeting.

APRIL 23: John Denver.

APRIL 26: Boxing on closed circuit television: George Foreman versus five opponents.

MAY 2: Alice Cooper.

MAY 10: Frank Sinatra. Shows at 8 p.m. and midnight. This was one of the great concerts in Gardens history and the first to begin at midnight. Top ticket price was $25.00. Almost 36,000 people saw Sinatra, a building record for one man in one day.

MAY 11: Toronto Marlboros won the Memorial Cup for the seventh time, a Canadian record, in Thunder Bay, defeating Fort William.

MAY 17: East Indian concert: The Latamukesh Show.

JUNE 17-18: The Rolling Stones. The best tickets went for $10.00.

JUNE 30: Boxing on closed circuit television: Muhammad Ali beat Joe Bugner for the World Heavyweight Title; Carlos Monza beat Tony

Licata for the World Middleweight Title, and Victor Galindez fought Jorge Ahumada in a non-title bout.

JULY 19: Yes concert.

JULY 21: Olympic class women's volleyball: Canada, USA, Japan, Russia.

AUGUST 9: Todd Rundgren.

AUGUST 17: International boxing: Canada's Olympic Team versus Russia's Olympic Team.

SEPTEMBER 1: Jefferson Starship.

SEPTEMBER 5: The Doobie Brothers.

SEPTEMBER 10: Darryl Sittler chosen eleventh Leaf Captain.

SEPTEMBER 27: Real Thing on Ice: Canada's top figure skaters in an Olympic preview, organized by Toller Cranston.

SEPTEMBER 29: The Bee Gees.

SEPTEMBER 30: Boxing on closed circuit television: Muhammad Ali versus Joe Frazier. Top ticket price was $20.00. Ali won.

OCTOBER 7: Jethro Tull.

OCTOBER 8: Festival Italiano, featuring Claudio Villa.

OCTOBER 11: Leafs hockey opener: Toronto defeated Chicago 2-1. The season was opened by Hon. Pauline McGibbon, Lieutenant-Governor of Ontario, assisted by Harold Ballard.

OCTOBER 16: Rick Wakeman.

OCTOBER 27: Rod Stewart and The Faces.

NOVEMBER 4: World gymnastics: Milk Meet '75.

NOVEMBER 6-16: Ice Capades. A record gross set, nearly $632,000.

NOVEMBER 19: Isaac Hayes.

DECEMBER 12: Rolling Thunder Review, with Bob Dylan, Joan Baez, Jack Elliott and Bob Newwirth.

DECEMBER 11: The Who, an immediate sellout.

DECEMBER 18: International hockey: Moscow Selects versus Toronto Marlboros.

DECEMBER 23: Whipper Billy Watson Christmas Skate for Timmy.

1976

JANUARY 9: Z Z Top's Fandango.

JANUARY 13-25: Ice Follies. The January 25 show was seen by 14,850 people, the largest ice show crowd ever.

FEBRUARY 3: Mazowsze, Polish Song and Dance Company.

FEBRUARY 7: Darryl Sittler of the Toronto Maple Leafs scored six goals in one game against Boston and also had four assists to finish the night with ten points, an NHL record.

FEBRUARY 13: Toronto Star-Maple Leaf Indoor Games.

MARCH 5: Toronto Police Association concert with the Toronto Symphony Orchestra and the Police Choir, under the direction of Lieutenant-Colonel Clifford Hunt, C.B.E.

MARCH 14: Royal Marines and The Black Watch.

MARCH 30: Timmy Tyke Hockey Night of Champions.

APRIL 1: Genesis.

APRIL 11: Festival Di Primavera.

APRIL 18: Bad Company, with Styx.

APRIL 20: Supertramp.

APRIL 24: Royal Lipizzan Stallions.

APRIL 26: Kiss.

MAY 1: Frank Sinatra.

MAY 9: Paul McCartney and Wings.

MAY 10: Joe Cocker.

MAY 13: Johnny Winter.

MAY 27: Santana.

MAY 28: Bicentennial Cup Soccer on closed circuit television: England versus Italy.

JUNE 11: Olympic Benefit Concert, with Gordon Lightfoot, Sylvia Tyson, Murray McLaughlin and Liona Boyd.

JUNE 15: Boxing on closed circuit television: The Gladiators — George Foreman versus Joe Frazier. Foreman won by knockout in the fifth round.

JUNE 25: Live martial arts mixed match, with boxing on closed circuit television: Muhammad Ali versus Antonio Inoki. They fought to a draw.

JULY 3-4: Latvian Song Festival.

AUGUST 8: Frank Tunney's pro wrestling: The Sheik versus Gene Kiniski.

AUGUST 11: Bay City Rollers.

AUGUST 13-14: International Roller Skating Tournament.

AUGUST 18: Loggins and Messina.

AUGUST 23-29: General Motors 1977 New Model Presentation.

SEPTEMBER 3: Canada Cup of Hockey: Sweden versus USA.

SEPTEMBER 5: Canada Cup of Hockey: Finland versus Czechoslovakia.

SEPTEMBER 7: Canada Cup of Hockey: Canada versus Sweden.

SEPTEMBER 8-10: Ford Motor Company 1977 New Model Presentation.

SEPTEMBER 11: Canada Cup of Hockey: Canada versus USSR.

SEPTEMBER 13: Canada Cup of Hockey playoff. Top price was $15.00.

SEPTEMBER 14: Electric Light Orchestra.

SEPTEMBER 16: Nazareth, with Mahogany Rush.

SEPTEMBER 23-24: The Ice Show, with Toller Cranston. Top price was $8.00, and for one performance no ice show has drawn better to this date.

SEPTEMBER 28: Boxing on closed circuit television: World Heavyweight Championship between Muhammad Ali and Ken Norton. Ali won.

OCTOBER 3: East Indian concert, with Kishore Kumar.

OCTOBER 5: Jackson Browne.

OCTOBER 10: Festival Italiano, with Rita Pavone and Little Tony.

OCTOBER 13: Leafs NHL hockey opener: the Leafs versus Boston. Joe Primeau, the only

living member of the "Kid Line," dropped the puck to open the season.

OCTOBER 15: Jeff Beck.

OCTOBER 16: Lanny McDonald scored three goals in fifty-four seconds, a club record.

OCTOBER 19: Paul Anka, featuring Odia Coates, with music by Johnny Harris. Top price was $25.00.

OCTOBER 21: The Who.

OCTOBER 22: Neil Diamond.

OCTOBER 25: Charley Pride, with Ronnie Prophet, Dave and Sugar and The Pridesmen.

NOVEMBER 2: Gymnastics: Milk Meet '76.

NOVEMBER 4-14: Ice Capades.

NOVEMBER 15: Doobie Brothers.

NOVEMBER 16: Frank Zappa.

NOVEMBER 21: Italian show, with Villa-Cugini.

NOVEMBER 24: Toronto Star-Maple Leaf Grand Prix, a showcase for Olympic riders.

NOVEMBER 29: The Bee Gees, featuring The Frank Carillo Band.

NOVEMBER 30: Robin Trouer.

DECEMBER 10: The Strawbs.

DECEMBER 29: Whipper Billy Watson Christmas Skate for Timmy.

DECEMBER 31: Rush concert.

1977

Harold Ballard receives the Timmy Award in 1977, is elected to the Hockey Hall of Fame and buys the Hamilton Tiger Cats.

JANUARY 3: Rush concert.

JANUARY 16: The Beach Boys.

JANUARY 18-30: Ice Follies. Record gross of $700,000.

FEBRUARY 1: Queen concert.

FEBRUARY 6: Frank Tunney's pro wrestling: Terry Funk lost to Harley Race for the World Championship, with special referee Pat

O'Connor; U.S. title match between The Sheik and Bobo Brazil.

FEBRUARY 11: Toronto Star-Maple Leaf Indoor Games.

FEBRUARY 13: Bruce Springsteen.

FEBRUARY 14: Fiftieth anniversary of the Toronto Maple Leafs.

FEBRUARY 22: Hockey: private school tournament. At 2 p.m. Appleby College Seniors versus Lakefield Seniors, 3:30 p.m. saw the colleges' junior teams play. In the evening, the Leafs and Buffalo played. In attendance was His Royal Highness Prince Andrew, who also visited the Leaf dressing room.

MARCH 3-4: Adidas Tri-Country Track Meet: Canada, USA, USSR. Twenty-fifth anniversary of Hockey Night in Canada.

MARCH 6: Genesis.

MARCH 8: Santana.

MARCH 22: Peter Gabriel.

MARCH 24: Jethro Tull.

MARCH 25: Catholic Youth Organization hockey.

MARCH 30: The Eagles.

APRIL 4: Electric Light Orchestra.

APRIL 11: Timmy Tyke Hockey Tournament.

APRIL 18: Al Stewart.

APRIL 24: Domenico Modugno Show.

APRIL 29: The Kinks.

MAY 1: Boston concert.

MAY 6-8: Shriners' Circus.

JUNE 1-2: Supertramp.

JUNE 12: Ted Nugent, with Uriah Heep.

JUNE 16: Hall and Oates.

JUNE 21: Blue Oyster Cult, with Todd Rundgren.

AUGUST 9: Bob Marley and the Wailers.

AUGUST 15: Peter Frampton.

AUGUST 27: East Indian concert: Ashe Bosle and Group.

SEPTEMBER 4-18: General Motors 1978 New Model Introduction.

SEPTEMBER 22: The Ice Show, with Toller Cranston.

SEPTEMBER 25: East Indian concert, with Mohamad Rafi and Party.

SEPTEMBER 29: Frank Zappa.

SEPTEMBER 30: Grenadier Guards and Scots Guards bands.

OCTOBER 2: Italian music show, starring Cocciante.

OCTOBER 5-9: Moscow Circus. The circus brought in the biggest gross in Gardens' history.

OCTOBER 12: Rod Stewart.

OCTOBER 15: NHL opener for the Leafs against Buffalo; Buffalo won 5-2. The season was opened by Clarence Campbell, President of the NHL. Darryl Sittler finished this season with a team record 117 points.

OCTOBER 24: Steve Miller.

OCTOBER 30: Italian show, with Franco Franchi.

OCTOBER 31: Chicago concert.

NOVEMBER 1: International gymnastics: the Ontario Cup, sponsored by Coca Cola.

NOVEMBER 3-13: Ice Capades.

NOVEMBER 21: Queen concert.

NOVEMBER 22: Toronto Star-Maple Leaf International Grand Prix.

NOVEMBER 24: Gino Vannelli.

DECEMBER 1: Billy Joel.

DECEMBER 10: Aerosmith.

DECEMBER 28: Christmas Skate for Timmy.

DECEMBER 30: Rush concert.

1978

JANUARY 2: International hockey: Toronto Maple Leafs versus Czechoslovakia. This was the first time the Leafs had played a European team.

JANUARY 5: Bob Hope and Friends, with Buddy Rogers, Phil Crosby, Les Brown and his Orchestra. This was one of the great shows at the Gardens, with tickets as high as $100. The Charlie Conacher Cancer Research Fund was the beneficiary.

JANUARY 17-29: Ice Follies.

FEBRUARY 2-3: Emerson, Lake and Palmer.

FEBRUARY 10: Toronto Star-Maple Leaf Indoor Games.

FEBRUARY 16: Santana.

MARCH 9: Blue Oyster Cult.

MARCH 10: Toronto Police Association concert, with Tony Bennett. Top price was $25.00.

MARCH 17: Jimmy Buffett.

MARCH 19: World Figure Skating Tour.

MARCH 21: Triumph.

MARCH 26: Timmy Tyke Hockey Tournament.

APRIL 2-4: Shriners' Circus.

APRIL 9: Eric Clapton.

APRIL 12: The Tubes concert.

MAY 1: David Bowie.

MAY 3: Nazareth.

MAY 20: Bob Seger.

JUNE 3-4: Red Foster's Ontario Floor Hockey Games.

JUNE 9: Bob Marley and the Wailers.

JUNE 11-14: Metro Toronto Billy Graham Crusade.

JUNE 17: East Indian concert, starring Noor Jehan.

JUNE 19: Ted Nugent.

JULY 2: Lithuanian Song Festival.

JULY 17: Crosby, Stills and Nash.

JULY 25: Leo Sayer.

JULY 30-31: Neil Diamond.

AUGUST 6: East Indian concert, with Kishnore Kumar.

AUGUST 19: Linda Ronstadt.

AUGUST 21: Boston concert.

SEPTEMBER 19-22: Ford Motor Company 1979 Introduction of New Models.

OCTOBER 1: Neil Young.

OCTOBER 3: Frank Zappa.

OCTOBER 5: Billy Joel.

OCTOBER 8: Festival Italiano, starring Mino Feitano.

OCTOBER 12: Bob Dylan.

OCTOBER 14: Leafs NHL hockey opener: the Leafs defeated the Islanders 10-7, with Darryl Sittler scoring seven points. The season was opened by Whipper Billy Watson and the two Timmies of the year, Peter and Paul Settle of Hamilton.

OCTOBER 15: Jethro Tull.

OCTOBER 16: Peter Gabriel.

OCTOBER 20: Donna Summer.

NOVEMBER 1: Al Stewart.

NOVEMBER 2-12: Ice Capades.

NOVEMBER 13: Grease concert.

NOVEMBER 14: International gymnastics: Ontario Cup '78.

NOVEMBER 16: Bruce Springsteen.

NOVEMBER 27: Ten C.C. concert.

NOVEMBER 30: Moody Blues.

DECEMBER 3: Queen concert.

DECEMBER 8: Bob Seger.

DECEMBER 17: Frank Tunney's pro wrestling: Whipper Billy Watson appreciation night. Rick "Nature Boy" Flair versus Ricky Steamboat; Gene Kiniski versus Dino Bravo.

DECEMBER 28, 29, 31: Rush concert.

1979

JANUARY 16-28: Ice Follies, featuring Peggy Fleming and Richard Dwyer.

FEBRUARY 2: Toronto Star-Maple Leaf Indoor Games.

MARCH 18: Santana and Eddie Money.

MARCH 19: Trooper.

MARCH 30: Harlem Globetrotters. Attendance record of 16,850 set for basketball.

APRIL 13: Timmy Tyke Hockey Tournament.

APRIL 20: Yes concert.

APRIL 23: Village People.

APRIL 25: Gino Vannelli.

MAY 6-7: Rod Stewart: Blondes Have More Fun, World Tour '79.

MAY 9: Liberal Party rally, with Prime Minister Pierre Trudeau.

MAY 11: Toronto Police Association concert, featuring Alma Faye Brooks, Lisa Dal Bello, Bob McBride.

MAY 15: Van Halen.

MAY 25-27: Garden Bros. Circus.

JUNE 12: Cheap Trick.

JUNE 14: The Cars concert.

JUNE 22: Max Webster.

JUNE 28-JULY 4: Kiwanis International Convention.

JULY 4: Punch Imlach back as Leafs' General Manager.

JULY 29: Steve Martin.

AUGUST 4: Kiss concert.

AUGUST 25-26: Church of Jesus of Latter Day Saints area conference.

AUGUST 31: The Bee Gees.

SEPTEMBER 9: Frank Tunney's pro wrestling: Canadian Heavyweight Championship tournament.

SEPTEMBER 16-21: Training camp for the Toronto Maple Leafs. It was traditional for the team to train elsewhere.

OCTOBER 5: Jethro Tull.

OCTOBER 7: ABBA.

OCTOBER 10: Leafs NHL opener: New York Rangers defeated Toronto 6-3. The season was opened by His Eminence G. Emmett Cardinal

Carter, the first time a religious figure had done so.

OCTOBER 11: Earth, Wind and Fire.

OCTOBER 12: Little River Band.

OCTOBER 18-19: Styx.

NOVEMBER 1: Bob Marley and the Wailers.

NOVEMBER 6-11: Ice Capades.

1980

JANUARY 11: Aerosmith concert.

JANUARY 15-27: Ice Follies. Ice Follies had been bought by Ringling Bros. Barnum and Bailey Circus for $12,000,000. Richard Dwyer did not have his old responsibilities, but he skated well.

FEBRUARY 1: Toronto Star-Maple Leaf Indoor Games. Prices were now $13.00 tops. Eamon Coghlan of Ireland won the mile race for the fifth straight time.

FEBRUARY 22-24: Garden Bros. Circus. This Canadian circus took in nearly $400,000 in three days.

MARCH 12: During a Maple Leaf-St. Louis NHL hockey game a nude man streaked across the ice, another first at Maple Leaf Gardens.

MARCH 20: The Metropolitan Toronto Police Association 61st Annual Concert, starring Marty Robbins, Hank Williams, Jr., Gene Watson and Eddie Eastman.

MARCH 21: John Denver.

MARCH 23: The NHL Oldtimers' game between the Montreal Canadiens and the Toronto Maple Leafs. It was probably the greatest Oldtimers' game in history. Harold Ballard gave the Gardens over to the use of charity. Around $200,000 was raised for Canadian Special Olympics, the Wellesley Cancer Hospital, the Charlie Conacher Research Fund and McDonald House. An entire page of Maple Leaf Gardens' 1981 calendar was devoted to the game.

MARCH 28: Hockey: Toronto Dominion Bank versus Radio Station CKEY, with proceeds going to the Toronto Sick Children's Hospital. In 1980 the entire Leaf team visited the Hospital for Sick Children just before Christmas.

MARCH 29: Edmonton beat Toronto 8-5 with nineteen-year old Wayne Gretzky taking over NHL scoring leadership. Someone threw three mice on the ice.

APRIL 3: Z Z Top Concert.

APRIL 11: Toronto was eliminated by Minnesota in Stanley Cup play, the second expansion team after Philadelphia to do so.

APRIL 6: April Wine and Johnny Winter. Lee Major, the Six Million Dollar Man, came to the Gardens and bought a Leaf sweater on this day.

APRIL 23: Jimmy Connors, wearing a Leaf sweater, and Ilie Nastase, wearing a Montreal sweater, played tennis before 11,000 fans. Cathy Jordan and Marjorie Blackwood played some tennis on the distaff side. Special celebrity seats sold for $50 each.

APRIL 27: The Beach Boys. Tom Shipley and Mike Brewer did the introductory act. Both Shipley and Brewer had been at the Gardens previously with Jethro Tull.

MAY 5 and 6: The Who concert. One of the big ones. They had just appeared on the cover of *Time* magazine. Both shows were sold out immediately.

JUNE 3: Nazareth. When asked what side of the Clyde River they came from they answered, "There's only one side."

JUNE 16: Little River Band from Australia.

JUNE 20: On the giant screen from Montreal: the World Welterweight Championship between Sugar Ray Leonard and Roberto Duran. Duran won a fifteen-round decision. Even though it was on the giant screen, from this fight derived the biggest boxing gross in Toronto history, about $250,000. Two well known fans, Charles Templeton and Pierre Berton, were in the crowd.

JUNE 21: Prism from Vancouver. Also on the programme were F.M. and Pump, two other western Canadian groups.

JUNE 23-24: Two successive days of Genesis. Both sold out. Two asteroid pinball machines were installed in their dressing room.

JULY 3: Peter Gabriel.

JULY 5-13: The Baptist World Congress. About 20,000 people came from all over the world and the famed evangelist Billy Graham addressed one of the meetings.

JULY 7: Joan Armatrading.

JULY 18: Van Halen.

JULY 28: AC/DC and Streetheart.

AUGUST 6: Kenny Loggins.

AUGUST 7: Journey.

AUGUST 9: Cheap Trick.

AUGUST 29: Yes concert.

SEPTEMBER 5: Ted Nugent. Humble Pie was a special guest.

SEPTEMBER 7: Elton John.

SEPTEMBER 14: The Toronto Maple Leafs began their 1980-81 training camp.

SEPTEMBER 21: An East Indian Concert with Melody Queen, Lata Mangeshkar and Manna Dey. Top priced tickets were $20.00.

SEPTEMBER 26: Triumph concert.

SEPTEMBER 28: Paul Simon.

OCTOBER 2: On the giant screen, Muhammad Ali attempted a comeback against Larry Holmes. The old Gardens' favourite was a sorry fighter. Top price was $20.00.

OCTOBER 11: The Toronto Maple Leafs began the 1980-81 NHL season with an opening 8-3 loss to the New York Rangers. Former Police Chief Harold Adamson dropped the puck for the official face-off and the 48th Highlanders Band was in attendance.

OCTOBER 19: Frank Tunney presented a Canadian Championship Wrestling Match with Dewey Robertson versus The Great Hossein Arab.

OCTOBER 24-26: World Cup Gymnastics. It was the first time that the World Cup was held in North America.

NOVEMBER 4-9: Ice Capades. Randy and Tia headlined the show. The Ice Capades had the Gardens to themselves because the Ice Follies dropped its run.

NOVEMBER 11: Frank Zappa.

NOVEMBER 16: Frank Tunney presented a World Title Wrestling Match between Harley Race and Rick "Nature Boy" Flair.

NOVEMBER 18: Death of Conn Smythe.

NOVEMBER 20-21: Another big rock show with Barry Manilow, called by some one of the great artists of 1980.

NOVEMBER 25: The return bout of Roberto Duran and Sugar Ray Leonard, this time from New Orleans. The top price was $25.00, and a box office record was created. Duran, like Ali in a previous Gardens' bout disappointed the crowd.

NOVEMBER 27: Once again indoor soccer was tried at the Gardens: the Toronto Blizzard played Calgary.

DECEMBER 31: The year closed out with the Max Webster concert.

1981

Maple Leaf Gardens began preparing to celebrate the first fifty years and enter the next half-century.

NOVEMBER 12: Fiftieth anniversary at the building.

Gardens Management

PRESIDENTS: J. P. Bickell, 1931-1937; George R. Cottrelle, 1937-1943; E. W. Bickle, 1943-1946; Conn Smythe, 1946-1961; Stafford Smythe, 1961-1969, 1970-1971; George Mara, 1969, 1970, 1971; Harold Ballard, 1971-present.

BUILDING SUPERINTENDENTS: Doug Morris, 1931-1963; Don MacKenzie, 1963-present.

PUBLICITY DIRECTORS: William Hewitt, 1931-1935; Frank Selke, 1931-1946; Ed Fitkin, 1945-1952, 1960-1966; Spiff Evans, 1946-1960; Stan Obodiac, 1959-present.

TREASURERS: B. Cody, Sid Hulbig, Len Heath, Bob Giroux, Don Crump.

BOX-OFFICE MANAGERS: Henry Bolton, 1931-1963; Jack Hoult, 1963-1969; Gordon Finn, 1969-present.

CONCESSION MANAGERS: Dick Dowling, Jack Hoult, Harry Sepp, Alex Patykewich.

CHIEF ENGINEERS: Sid Vincent, 1931-1956; Jack Gordon, 1956-1974; Doug Moore, 1974-present.

Index to the Text

206